MAKE
WORK
BETTER

MAKE
WORK
BETTER

Revolutionizing How Great Bosses Lead, Give Feedback, and Empower Employees

By
Doug Dennerline and Jamie Aitken
Foreword by Josh Bersin

Skyhorse Publishing

Skyhorse Publishing books may be purchased in bulk at special discounts for
sales promotion, corporate gifts, fund-raising, or educational purposes. Special
editions can also be created to specifications. For details, contact the Special Sales
Department, Skyhorse Publishing, 307 West 36th Street, 11th Floor, New York,
NY 10018 or info@skyhorsepublishing.com.

Skyhorse® and Skyhorse Publishing® are registered trademarks of Skyhorse
Publishing, Inc.®, a Delaware corporation.

Visit our website at www.skyhorsepublishing.com.

10 9 8 7 6 5 4 3 2 1

Library of Congress Cataloging-in-Publication Data is available on file.

Cover design by David Ter-Avanesyan

ISBN: 978-1-5107-7491-9
Ebook ISBN: 978-1-5107-7579-4

Printed in the United States of America

Contents

Foreword by Josh Bersin   vi

A Note to the Reader   viii

Introduction   ix

Chapter 1:   How We Manage Performance and Why It Sucks   1

Chapter 2:   Make Work Better with Performance Enablement   19

Chapter 3:   Performance Enablement from the Ground Up   41

Chapter 4:   Putting Performance Enablement into Practice with People Development Plans   59

Chapter 5:   Leading Your Performance Transformation   77

Chapter 6:   Implementing Performance Enablement   99

Chapter 7:   Scaling Your Initiative with Technology   115

Chapter 8:   Compensation   127

Conclusion   161

Appendix 1: What We Believe   165

Appendix 2: Performance Enablement in Action: Case Studies   169

Index   183

Notes   191

About the Authors   195

Foreword
by Josh Bersin

What Is The Real Management Secret To High Performance?

Managers have been trying to unlock the secrets of employee performance for decades. And unfortunately, driven by the legacy of the industrial age, we often rely on "performance management."

This dreaded phrase, which is widely discussed in every board room and HR department, comes with an enormous amount of baggage. In the 70s and 80s, every company copied GE, creating a "rank and yank" approach to force the bottom 10% out of the company every year. In the 90s, we focused on "continuous performance management" and feedback, trying to teach managers to coach, not lead. Today, as we enter a new decade, it's time to think about it once again, reflecting new ideas and new philosophies of leadership.

The bottom line, however, is pretty simple. Do you want performance management to "evaluate and manage-out" the low performers? Or do you want the process to develop, inspire, and challenge your people to do much more? As Doug and Jamie's book points out, the latter is by far the best approach.

And why is this so important? We've entered a period in the economy where human skills, innovation, and creative ways to solve problems almost always win out over "execution-focused" strategies. Yes, of course, every company needs to execute, but if we don't let every individual in the company bring their own talents to the job, "execution" feels uninspired and easy to copy.

In other words, this book is all about how to manage a company that grows. In my experience as an analyst and consultant, I've seen hundreds of companies that "execute" like a fine-tuned machine. But many of them (GE is a great example), suffer from lots of "coverups" and other fixes to make sure the "execution" goes in the right direction. And how do you avoid this from happening? You manage people as adults; you give them power and authority; and you "enable their performance" as a leader, manager, or supervisor.

This book explains how to do this. It's not really a book about "performance management," it's a book about "helping people perform." And that, regardless of what you think, is what performance management is all about.

HR leaders and CEOs need to realize it's time to take the plunge and move away from these archaic process that are over used today to something that will grow people and therefore attracts the best talent.

I hope you read the book carefully, dig into the stories, and use it as a manifesto. I know, from my own experience as a leader, manager, and analyst, that "helping people perform" will always get you into the right place.

Josh Bersin
Global Industry Analyst
Advisor to BetterWorks

A Note to the Reader

THIS BOOK IS a collaborative effort between Doug Dennerline, CEO of Betterworks, and Jamie Aitken, vice president of HR Transformation at Betterworks. Throughout the book, we refer to ourselves as the collective *we*, and when we share personal stories we will describe events in the third person, as in "When Doug worked at Cisco" or "When Jamie attended a human resources conference" to avoid confusion and clarify who is doing what. Though we speak from two very different perspectives and work histories—Doug as a CEO and Jamie as a human resources executive—we share a unified passion for making work better. We strongly believe that to do so requires CEOs and HR professionals to work together. When we looked for books that took both the CEO's and HR professional's perspective into consideration when rethinking and transforming performance management, we couldn't find one. So, we decided to write it ourselves. We knew we didn't just want to talk the talk but also to walk the walk, so we wrote this book as a team to show that when CEOs and HR executives come together, great things can happen—for their employees, the clients they serve, and their organizations as a whole.

Introduction

MANY OF US alive and working in 1995 couldn't say where we were on July 17. It was, for most, an unremarkable Monday. We got in our cars, drove the average thirty to sixty minutes to our corporate office jobs, showed our IDs to a security guard at the entrance, and grabbed our coffees at the coffeemaker with our company mug (Starbucks wasn't yet on every corner in the United States) before heading to the work area. As on every other workday, we entered our offices or cubicles, looked through the stack of files left on our desks the day before, and started pushing papers and heading to the first of many in-person meetings for the week. On our lunch breaks, we headed outside, ventured into a bookstore, scanned the shelves, and found something to read while we ate our packed lunch. For those of us who lived in a major city, we could find a Borders, where we might find the newest Michael Crichton, Mary Higgins Clark, or John Grisham book just hitting the shelves or sample Madonna's or Mariah Carey's latest CD.

Those not in the workforce (or not even born then) might not know that Borders was one of the world's biggest book and CD stores in its heyday. The Borders Group operated the second-largest bookstore chain (behind Barnes & Noble), had more than twelve hundred domestic and international stores, and employed about fifteen thousand people. Its revenue was $4 billion, and it didn't look like it would slow down anytime soon. Little did Borders know that while its aisles were filled with book buyers whiling away their lunch hour, just the day before, in a garage in Seattle, a man by the name of Jeff Bezos "opened" the world's first online bookstore, Amazon.

At first, Borders wasn't threatened by Amazon. But then, steadily, things began to change. More and more people skipped their bookstore visits, heading online to shop. While preoccupied with several other internal mismanagement issues, Borders's leaders simply couldn't fathom its buyers not wanting to shop in a brick-and-mortar store for their books. They were slow to adapt to the changing landscape and paid the price. People wanted convenience—they wanted the books to come to them. They were now getting used to that. They wanted to compare prices, give and get instant reviews on the books they were reading or considering, receive customized recommendations based on their previous shopping cart, and do it all from the comfort of their own homes. Borders couldn't see the big picture, and not only was their industry changing but also the entire world. By 2011 Borders, like the dinosaurs of the latest Michael Crichton book, ceased to exist.

While Borders was taking a nosedive in front of the world, Doug was an executive at Cisco. He watched the impact of the Internet on millions of companies like Borders that failed to reinvent themselves. Another shift is happening right now. So many people are going about their days as if nothing has changed. Yet, whether they are aware of it or not, the change we're undergoing will be just as disruptive as Amazon was to millions of businesses worldwide—the impact of which is making waves to this day, as other companies still scramble to adapt. It's not a company or a *what*, mind you, that's changing. It's a *how*; *how* people work. And if we don't reinvent the processes around how we manage people, the same thing that happened to Borders can happen to companies all over the world. Just like so many brick-and-mortar stores became obsolete, so will all the companies still operating under the archaic employee-management systems and use of annual performance reviews to manage employees. Employees will leave to find employers that are invested in their growth and careers and have built processes that support that.

About Betterworks: What We Do

In the next ten years, nearly 75 percent of the workforce will be millennials. They were raised *with* Amazon.com; many of them can't remember a time before. They are used to a world that responds to them, is in tune with them, and anticipates what they need.

They want convenience in their work. They want flexibility. They want to be evaluated at their jobs in ways that make sense to them. And they will not work for companies that use annual performance reviews or that track or monitor their every move with employee-monitoring software. Primarily, they want a simple and convenient performance-management tool.

In addition, the world has changed since the COVID-19 pandemic, which completely revolutionized how we work. Overnight, most of us switched to a work-from-home (WFH) model. As the pandemic lockdown progressed, we all realized we needed to adapt quickly. Even though we couldn't be at work in person, the work had to be done. So, we figured out how to have virtual meetings, to communicate throughout the day using various apps, and to adapt to hybrid work environments. Employees became used to this type of engagement, and many enjoyed the extra time they gained in the day without a commute. They found they were more productive and able to integrate work and life in their WFH offices. Many companies were shocked that they met resistance when they demanded people return to the office, especially among millennials and Gen Zers, who thrived during the pandemic and began to question their prepandemic work environments. They started to doubt the institutions for which they were working. They want to work for organizations with *their* best interests in mind.

Amazon has always been successful because it has always put the customers first, anticipating their needs, asking for feedback, and responding in kind. As a result, it gives their customers more of what they're interested in—and does so in real time. Amazon adapted itself, as a tool, from simply being an online bookstore to an application that people now rely on to buy *everything*. Its business model adapted to every demand of its customers. Amazon is now a logistics company, one that not only sells its products but delivers them as well. It is also one of the largest venues for small businesses, which use the Amazon platform to sell.

Successful companies do what Amazon did. They adapt, change, and grow with the times. But the *best* companies don't just focus on their customers; they focus internally on their employees as well. Richard Branson, billionaire founder of Virgin Group, famously said, "Clients do not come first, employees come first. If you take care of your employees, they will take care of your clients." Happy, engaged, and empowered employees are what make an organization go beyond being successful to being truly transformational. To be great, an organization has to rethink and transform how it engages with employees, or what is commonly called *performance management* or PM.

Instead of performance management, we prefer to call it *performance enablement*, which focuses on the following questions:

- What do I need as an employee to grow my career to develop as a professional?

- With my manager at my side, how do I lower internal and external barriers that prevent me from achieving my goals, both personally and professionally?

Instead of waiting a year for feedback at an annual performance review, employees want this feedback in real time throughout the year, so they can solve the problems getting in the way of their career growth and accomplish their goals today. Mind you, this is different than loading employee-monitoring software on their computers to see when they are working. Who would want to work for a company that distrusts its employees that way? Performance enablement is about regular check-ins with the manager, in which the employee drives the engagement as much as the manager. Lightweight check-ins with each other should be continuous, so employees are constantly engaged and know their work is helping their company achieve its goals.

Multiple–Trillion Dollar-Problems

Companies simply can't afford not to change their processes. Too much is at stake. Employees today don't want to wait for feedback, which they have little control over. Managers don't have the time to waste five weeks preparing annual performance reviews. We have been moving in this direction for decades; the COVID-19 pandemic just got us here faster. More employees are working from home—they don't even see their managers in person regularly. And as 2022 has shown us, unhappy employees will not wait for their companies to figure out what they're doing wrong. It costs companies trillions of dollars. According to the Gartner company, the US employee annual voluntary turnover jumped 20 percent this year, from a prepandemic annual average of 31.9 million employees quitting their jobs to

37.4 million quitting.[1] The cost of replacing an individual can range from one-half to two times the employee's annual salary, and that's being conservative. If a one-hundred-person organization provides an average salary of $50,000, then, with a turnover rate of 37.4 percent, replacing employees could cost up to $2.6 million a year—multiply that by every company in the United States, and that's a trillion-dollar problem.

But that's just the tip of the iceberg. What about those who stay? How can we make them want to stay and remain engaged? Another perennial problem faces managers and HR: How do you keep employees productive so that they achieve their goals? A trend advocates *quiet quitting*. Various interpretations and definitions of what it means to quiet quit exist. According to Kelsey Pelzer of Parade, it means doing the bare minimum of what's acceptable before punching out. Workers are not leaving their jobs, but they aren't participating in anything they perceive as out of scope. Whereas employees of all ages participate in some version of quiet quitting, Gen Z (individuals born anywhere from 1996 to 2012) have been the most vocal about it on social media. Although some workers want the paycheck while not working, quiet quitters don't seem to mind working. They're just not willing to sacrifice their life or private time to do any extra or off-the-clock work.[2]

They certainly have their reasons. According to Gallup's *State of the Global Workplace: 2022 Report*, employee stress is at an all-time high. In Gallup's summary video, it states, "The pulse of the global workplace is driven by well-being and engagement, and that pulse is dangerously low." According to its report, most employees do not find their work "meaningful or hopeful about the future."[3] In a list of key findings Gallup stated,

Employee well-being is the new workplace imperative. Well-being and engagement interact with each other in powerful ways. When employees are engaged and thriving, they experience significantly less stress, anger, and health problems. Unfortunately, most employees remain disengaged at work. In fact, low engagement alone costs the global economy $7.8 trillion.[4]

Some companies think the solution is spending millions on software that tracks clicks on a computer and the time spent in front of the laptop. That doesn't measure anything; worse, Big Brother oversight does not enable performance. It ultimately breeds contempt, stress, and, at worst, paranoia. None of it is conducive to achievement or outcomes. We believe that when there is agreement between a manager and their employees on both personal and professional goals, the employees are more engaged and goal-oriented and know their work matters and affects the overall success of the company. They don't need a Big Brother exercising total control over people's lives; they need to feel empowered.

New Rules of Managing Performance

We've seen companies we've worked with—Vertiv, Kroger, Colgate-Palmolive, University of Phoenix, Emerson Electric, Echelon Wealth Partners, PepsiCo, Intuit, and many more—performed better than companies that do things the old way. They're winning against their competitors, their stock is going up, and their revenues are growing faster because they have intentionally created environments where their people are working on the most important things and therefore have better experiences. They are engaged and getting immediate feedback, and their managers are interested in their career growth and helping them succeed. And they aren't the only ones. A 2020 Gartner poll showed that 87 percent of HR leaders were considering changes to performance reviews, and well over two-thirds of organizations make performance-management changes in any given year.[5]

These companies see the writing on the wall. Deloitte, in its white paper *Performance Management: Playing a Winning Hand* that looked at trends in how companies managed performance, found that the old rules no longer applied. New rules were in town. Instead of performance appraisals and goal-setting conducted once or twice a year, employees want check-ins conducted quarterly or more frequently with "regular goal-setting in an open and collaborative process." Instead of feedback by managers collected at the end of the year, they want to receive it "continuously" and be able to easily review it with transparent "apps and tools." Instead of goals being kept confidential with a focus on individual achievement, they want goals to be public and to have an increased focus on team achievement. Instead of managers evaluating employees only, employees want the opportunity to evaluate managers. Regarding compensation, employees no longer expect that information to be kept confidential or based on rating bands. Rather, they would like compensation levels to be transparent across the organization and based on their achievements. Most important, instead of managers focusing on "evaluating performance," they would be focused on coaching and developing their employees. And all this would be done using data while reducing biases.[6]

In addition to having more frequent and collaborative processes in place, being more transparent and balanced, and focusing more on coaching and developing skills toward a common goal, companies are also attempting to meet employees where they are. Just like Amazon brought the world to their customer's doorsteps, performance-enablement software brings the tool to both managers and employees. They interact with our software in the applications they live in the most, whether that's Salesforce if they're in sales, Jira if they're in engineering, or Gmail or Outlook for other roles. With a couple of keystrokes, employees can communicate with their managers and vice versa about their goals and problems, which is all transparent. Within minutes they can have an answer or encouragement or whatever they need at the moment.

Managers who spent up to five weeks completing annual performance reviews now take a few hours during each quarter to communicate, with more relevant real-time information. Employees, too, wasted precious time when they could have been productive. And more often than not, the goals they initially set for the year may no longer be relevant and should have been rewritten, yet their managers rated their performance based on the previous annual review. What a waste of time that is—for everyone. We believe managers should spend no more than fifteen minutes preparing the feedback to give to each employee during regular check-ins throughout the year. The process is about changing the culture around feedback so that it's both transparent and aligned with both the employee's and the organization's goals. The happiest, most productive, and most empowered employees are those who see that their daily goals and activities contribute meaningfully to the entire organization's goals.

Our Perspective

We feel so passionate about performance enablement and empowering leaders, HR, and employees that we are writing a book about it. We have spent our careers trying to find better processes to make work better, and we can finally share what we have discovered with the world.

Doug started working in 1982 for Hewlett-Packard. At the time, it was moving from mainframe computers to minicomputers—the PC had not become popular yet, and Amazon did not exist. Five years later, Doug fell into the world of networking and saw the potential impact of the Internet on the industry. He, too, went through all the performance-management and HR processes in the companies he worked for—Hewlett-Packard, 3Com Corporation, and Cisco Systems, where he had six thousand employees working for him. With his HR business partner, he saw firsthand how terrible the processes worked. He, and others who work in this industry, are shocked that, with the world at our fingertips viaphones, laptops, and applications, companies remain stuck in the past, using old processes and systems that should have been retired long ago. Even at advanced high-tech companies like Cisco, Doug saw antiquated performance-management processes and the negative impact they had on people. Cisco has since moved to a lightweight, new process for performance, and has one of the longest-tenured employee bases in the technology industry. As the CEO of Betterworks, where we make HR software designed with its users in mind—not just in HR, but leaders, managers, and employees—Doug and his team have spent years inventing a process that has a real impact on engagement, retention, and positive outcomes for companies brave enough to go through the change to get there.

Meanwhile, Jamie has been working in the HR space for over twenty-five years and has been passionately focused on helping people at work. Unfortunately, though, it hasn't always been easy. Over the years, she has attended numerous HR conferences, with one session at every conference titled, "Get Your Seat at the Table." Jamie often laughs when she says, "We're always trying to get a seat at the table and have our voices heard!" Jamie finds that HR's moment has finally arrived. HR professionals and CEOs working together have a unique opportunity to fundamentally shift how work is done. It's the perfect storm for HR. The turnover rate is at an all-time high. Influencers tell people to quiet quit—all while production demand is only growing and the need for engaged, driven, and goal-oriented employees is higher than ever. *Now is the time* for HR to assertively contribute to how businesses are operated and how employees are taken care of.

What You Can Expect

Make Work Better: Revolutionizing How Great Bosses Lead, Give Feedback, and Empower Employees will show you how to do those very things. In the following pages, we'll highlight real-life case studies from our clients—Intuit, Vertiv, PepsiCo, Colgate-Palmolive, Rivian, Optimizely—and more. We'll show you what's not working and why work sucks and clearly explain what it costs your company. We'll also offer real solutions. We'll break down how to rethink performance enablement so the emphasis will be on transparent quarterly goal-setting, increased frequency of check-ins between managers and direct reports, structured and unstructured feedback times, and consistent recognition for work well done, and we'll highlight the importance of using data to make the right decisions and eliminate bias. We'll discuss how ratings work and make a case for eliminating them and discon-necting them from raises and promotions. We'll also highlight why giving those HR folks a seat at the table is so important (and not just because we said so—data backs us up).

Of course, we'll show how our software works and how it's different from other applications and PM programs on the market, but this isn't a book to sell you on Betterworks applications. Rather, we're advocating for all companies everywhere—and their employees. We just happen to have been studying performance enablement up close, watching its massive impacts on our clients. You could say we know a thing or two about performance management and can't wait to share what we've found. By the end of reading this book, we hope you're as inspired and passionate as we are about revolutionizing how you lead, give feedback, and empower employees to *make work better*.

Key Takeaways

- Feedback conversations don't have to occur in an annual review and don't have to happen constantly. They have to happen in a collaborative and relevant way so that it matches both the work and career goals.
- Frequent, lightweight conversations, which don't require exhaustive amounts of prep from either managers or employees and focus on personal and career development goals, in addition to work product, ensure that employees are engaged and feel supported.
- If your process and tools for feedback don't support or enable people to get their work done, then you aren't managing performance; you're impeding it.

CHAPTER 1

How We Manage Performance and Why It Sucks

How We Even Got Here

When sitting down to start filling out the much-begrudged annual performance review, most HR leaders and employees will likely lament the entire bureaucratic process. HR people know it sucks. Employees know it sucks and that it doesn't change performance. And yet, they do it. Many are not even sure why, other than the hackneyed excuse "This is the way we've always done it." What few people know is that it is indeed a *bureaucratic process,* conceived by one of the largest bureaucracies in the world, the US War Department—all the way back in 1920. After World War I, the United States military departments felt they needed a formal evaluation of their officers and introduced the Efficiency Report. As the name suggests, it measures an officer's efficiency.

By 1922, the departments rebranded the report as the WD AGO Form, and it was expanded to assess enlisted soldiers and their potential to become officers. The officers and enlisted soldiers weren't just being evaluated for their efficiency but in the "domains of physical qualities, intelligence, leadership, personal qualities, and general value to the service" as well. It was created by and large because military leaders struggled to adopt a fair process that compared officers. Essentially, this version was designed to include what is known as a "forced distribution rating system." That is, the form's purpose was to divide officers up by ranks and was meant to decrease promotions. Why would the military want to do that? The War Department faced a perennial issue within its branches: too many promotions. That year, the US Navy claimed that most of its officers were rated in the top 1 percent. The math didn't add up. How could nearly every officer be in the top 1 percent? The War Department hoped to force a distribution of decreased ratings and help it focus on who deserved a promotion and who needed more training and, most important, where officers were best utilized according to their talents. It also hoped to do what it hadn't been successfully able to—flag and dismiss poor performers.[1]

With little fanfare, the US War Department unwittingly started what we now know as the annual performance review. After World War II, men left the US armed forces and entered civilian life—working in and even leading or starting new companies. Unsurprisingly, these men thought they knew a thing or two about managing performance. After all, they had served in the US military branches and grown accustomed to how the military evaluated employees through annual performance reviews. As a result, by the mid-1950s, 60 percent of US companies used annual appraisals to document workers' performance and allocate rewards. By the end of the 1960s, that number grew to nearly 90 percent.[2]

Social psychologists like Douglas McGregor joined the conversation shortly after. He argued in his seminal book *The Human Side of Enterprise* that if nearly all employees were expected to perform and would be measured on said performance, they would need obvious goals. Not long after, General Electric began to focus on development, separating the discussion of an employee's personal and professional growth from their accountability and goals.

But the world began to change in the eighties. As inflation rates skyrocketed, employers began to feel the heat from their employees. They were demanding higher pay and wanted to be rewarded for their performance. So out went personal growth and development, and back came accountability and the ability to reach company goals as a means to reward merits. By the 1990s, Jack Welch, the head of General Electric, took his show on the road, publicly championing his forced ranking system that awarded top performers. He essentially created the present-day annual performance review, where the top performers were the "best of the best" and were rewarded handsomely; those massed in the middle were given a small raise to be maintained, with the message that if they didn't do better work they'd be let go; and those at the bottom were let go or managed out of the organization.

With the dawn of tech companies and a shifting work landscape, organizations became less hierarchical in the late 1990s and early 2000s. As organizations flattened, a new problem arose. In 1998 *McKinsey Quarterly* published its groundbreaking "War for Talent" study that sent shock waves through multiple industries. The magazine's intensive study looked at seventy-seven of the largest companies in various industries and grouped them into sectors to compare the high performers with average players in their respective markets. Next, the researchers talked directly to the top two hundred or so executives in each of the high-performance companies, to understand the reasons they work where they do and how they became professionals (5,679 respondents). What they found was "a call to arms for corporate America."

Their research concluded that companies were about to be engaged in a "war for senior executive talent that will remain a defining characteristic of their competitive landscape for decades to come." Through their interviews, they found most senior executives were ill-prepared. Many had learned the skills needed decades prior but failed to keep up with the changing landscape of work and didn't have the skills required to lead their companies into the future. *McKinsey Quarterly* stated, "You can win the war for talent, but first you must elevate talent management to be a burning corporate priority." The way they believed an organization could do that was to "attract and retain the best people" and "create and perpetually refine an employee value proposition." Above all, the magazine found that the best way to recruit and retain great talent who would be prepared for this changing landscape was to "develop, develop, develop!"[3]

Still reeling from a talent shortage, by 2011 organizations were faced with another crisis. This time it wasn't just talent development; there were too many direct reports for each manager. Not only were managers and leaders in need of development themselves, but they also didn't have the time or resources to develop those under them. Too many people needed managing, and not enough hours were in the day.

Here we are in 2022: For the past twenty years, companies have been facing dramatic changes, a desperate need for talent, and not enough people to manage and develop upcoming talent, all the while using the same process to evaluate and manage their employees. We've faced a global pandemic and the Great Resignation, which, according to new studies, isn't projected to slow down. In 2021 nearly forty-eight million employees resigned from their jobs.[4] Employees are fed up and not sticking around for organizations to figure this out. As the character Howard Beale made clear in the iconic and prescient 1976 movie *Network*, employees are still mad, desperate for meaning, and want to be seen and heard: "I'm a human being! . . My life has value!" And forty-six years later, they're still shouting from the proverbial rooftops: "I am mad as hell, and I am not going to take it anymore!" Only they aren't just yelling; they're doing something much more damaging—they're voting with their feet, walking away in record numbers. And they aren't leaving quietly. They are giving their reasons on TikTok, Instagram, Facebook, and Twitter and publishing I-quit videos on YouTube. Then they're going on Glassdoor and saying: "Don't come and work here; it's all hat no cattle! [That is, all talk and no action.] This place sucks. The leaders have no idea what they're doing." Eventually, organizations will find it more challenging to attract the talent they need to stay relevant and competitive.

Rank-and-Yank System

New data from Gallup reveals that the performance reviews and rating systems that have been used by employers over the past decade are not having the effect they had hoped.[5] Instead of improved performance, companies have seen both a marked decline and dissatisfaction among employees. One company that saw this trend and reversed course was Microsoft Corporation. In November 2013 it sent shock waves through the corporate world when it announced that it was ending its "hated stack ranking," the employee-review and compensation system that it had established just two years prior. In this type of performance review, employees received one rating based on their manager's assessment ranging from one (highest) to five (lowest).[6] Thus the practice became commonly referred to as "rank and yank" because those who were lumped in the stack of underperformers were often fired or "encouraged to leave."

The ranking created massive internal contention among managers and their reports alike. Many managers struggled with this process because they felt they were forced to select a percentage of fives. It's often random and baseless (with a few exceptions). Doug remembers when he was in a company that did stack rankings and had to randomly pick people for each rank. Having had six thousand people in his organization and at best only one or two conversations with a person over the year, it was impossible to rank them accurately. It places a difficult burden on managers, and it makes employees distrust the system on which their career aspirations rest. Over time, it creates an unhealthy environment where people compete with each other—out of fear of being yanked—rather than support each other and the goals of the company. Microsoft saw how this process was affecting its culture and removed the practice. Nevertheless, most companies didn't follow suit. In fact, many doubled down and came out swinging, arguing that rank and yank was the only way to go. Not surprisingly, former General Electric CEO and longtime champion of stack ratings Jack Welch defended the process and argued that the term "rank and yank" was a "media-invented, politicized, sledgehammer of a pejorative that perpetuates a myth about a powerfully effective real practice called (more appropriately) differentiation."[7] We disagree.

F*** This

This year Goldman Sachs announced that layoffs were inevitable, and it reported that one way it was going to make those cuts was by using the annual performance review. Faced with a decline of 41 percent in quarterly earnings, CFO Denis Coleman called to tighten its belt.

This is a euphemism for what is commonly known as Strategic Role Assessment (SRA), which often calls for firing the bottom performers. Historically, when organizations do this, they yank about 5 percent of their employees. For Goldman Sachs, this equates to twenty-three hundred employees. Is it possible that twenty-three hundred bad performers are in a company? And if so, what does that say about the hiring process, management, and internal training and coaching? Instead of answering these questions, belt-tightening executives turn to performance reviews to answer the question of who should go.

Two former employees for Goldman Sachs, interviewed by the *Insider,* reported the intense annual 360 performance-review process was a "stressful, labor-intensive rite of passage in which employees solicit feedback from their colleagues about factors such as how effectively they embody the firm's culture and exhibit mindfulness about risk." In fact, the former employees asked to be kept anonymous. Even without the threat of being fired, these employees watched their backs. In many ways, we can empathize and see why the process was so traumatizing. Employees were required to identify as many as eight reviewers to vouch for them and rate them on a scale of one to ten. "Giving colleagues anything below a seven was considered a death knell," one ex-employee said. "If you gave anyone less than a seven on their [ratings], you really threw them under the bus. You really didn't give people less than a seven unless you really wanted to screw them." After weeks of gathering reviews and preparing for the actual in-person, behind-closed-door meeting, employees finally were able to sit down with their boss and hear what those they asked to review them had to say. Then in a separate meeting, after several other behind-closed-door conversations without the employee, bonus compensation was discussed. That meeting sometimes became contentious, even volatile.

One employee recalled a peer storming out of the meetings with managers and shouting, "Fuck this."[8]

The biggest failure of this kind of performance management is that we're ultimately setting organizations up to have an f***-this mindset. If people know that the system is designed to rank and yank, they are less likely to share where they need help or speak up about their goals. The primary goals of performance management should be to align employees' goals with strategic objectives and enable meaningful work, transparency, honesty, and accountability. Any process—namely, an annual performance review—that takes employees away from their meaningful work is what we would consider a tax on the employee (and, ultimately, the organization that he or she works for). We want to make the value of the process greater than the tax of it.

You're Just Not Creative Enough—We're Going to Let You Go

About a century ago, a young, ambitious, and hardworking artist just returning from World War I dreamed of becoming a cartoonist at a newspaper. The kid had chops. He could draw and had no shortage of ideas. At least that was his point of view and that of his friends who enjoyed his clever drawings and characters. But his boss at the local newspaper didn't share the same sentiments. After all, art can be a highly subjective endeavor. That same boss unceremoniously dismissed the young man, telling him the reason he was letting him go was "he lacked imagination and had no good ideas." Fortunately, that young man didn't listen to his boss. He took his creative talents elsewhere and he went on to create a little company called Disney.

Walt Disney is hardly alone. Many successful stories of world-famous entrepreneurs, innovators, industry leaders, and creatives began with someone underestimating, not understanding, or simply outright dismissing them. The stories are now legendary and shared far and wide. Mark Cuban was fired from a job as a computer salesman. Steve Jobs was famously ousted from the company he founded. The famous *Vogue* editor Anna Wintour clashed with her editor at her first job as a junior fashion editor for *Harper's Bazaar*. He thought she was "too edgy" and fired her after just nine months. No one even told Jerry Seinfeld he was fired when he showed up for a table read-through for a show from which his lines had been cut. Oprah Winfrey's first producer told her she was "unfit for television news" and removed her from her post.

Sometimes bosses don't know best. Sure, all of these icons landed on their feet. Many articles and essays about not giving up use these stories as examples of "look where they are now!" They all turned a bad experience into a positive one, and it makes for a nice feel-good story. But you don't see many essays or articles that focus on the bosses or organizations that let them go. They were the big losers in the stories. Whether it was Thomas Edison's schoolteacher who thought he would be nothing more than an idiot his whole life or Walt Disney's first boss who couldn't appreciate his creativity, they failed to recognize the capabilities, potential, or talents of the person standing before them. And what about the stories we don't hear? What happened to the people who don't become Oprah Winfrey, Jerry Seinfeld, or Mark Cuban? Where are they now? Were they all terrible at their jobs, underperformers, slackers, or just not in the right field or position?

Every year in performance reviews, bosses, managers, and leaders take their best guesses, and it's causing far more harm than good. Managers and their direct reports loathe and dread the traditional annual performance review. As a standalone exercise, devoid of context and supporting activity throughout the year, it is also tedious and time-consuming, and it can feel like an inquisition or an assault.

Because the process is considered so miserable, many employees would tell you they want *less* performance assessment, not more. But what they really don't want is the rank-and-yank system of the annual performance reviews.

What It Costs to Keep Doing Things the Old Way

Most people using the one-hundred-year-old performance review had zero input on its creation, yet they do it (begrudgingly) every year. Not surprisingly, annual performance reviews have been proven ineffective in changing behavior, improving outcomes, or attaining goals. But don't just take our word for it. A 2019 Gallup study showed that it costs organizations as much as $2.4 million to $35 million a year in lost working hours for an organization of ten thousand employees to engage in performance evaluations—with very little to show for it.[9] Moreover, regardless of what process or system is in place, the manager is in trouble if only one conversation happens a year about performance; the same poll found that such feedback is "unlikely to be meaningful." In contrast, the poll found that when employees receive frequent, honest feedback and the review is consistent with what they have heard all year, the feedback can "be affirming, motivating and, at the very least, much less awkward."

Gallup also found the following when managers provide continuous (vs. annual) feedback:

- Team members are 5.2 times more likely to strongly agree that they receive meaningful feedback.
- Employees are 3.2 times more likely to strongly agree they are motivated to do outstanding work.
- The workers are 2.7 times more likely to be engaged at work.

Gallup also agreed with what we have found when working with clients like Colgate-Palmolive. The best way to get performance-management (what we call performance-enablement) systems to work is to create a culture in which honest feedback can be given in a safe environment without employees feeling threatened. This all may take some time. It also means working with your entire organization on a shared definition of goals and performance ratings—that is, what constitutes excellence. And, of course, a company needs leaders who model what makes a great manager.

We speak of radical transparency, which implies radical candor,[10] or the ability to have difficult conversations, privately and publicly. We've found that when managers and employees are unable to have honest conversations with each other, the result is unhappy employees. Gallup's poll backs this up. When employees receive false praise and encouragement and are not given the tools they need to achieve their goals continuously throughout the year, or when their goals are misaligned with the company's goals, they feel they are being set up to fail. And, indeed, they often end up failing. And those costs, which are not just monetary, can add up quickly. They can be devastating to an organization.

Performance Reviews Tied to Compensation Create Toxic Cultures

The statistics over the past decade support Microsoft's decision. According to Gallup, only 14 percent of employees strongly agree that performance reviews inspire them to improve and perform. As Gallup states, "If performance reviews were a drug, they would not meet FDA approval for efficacy." If it is so ineffective, why do companies keep throwing good money after bad? It defies logic.

According to Jim Clifton and Jim Harter's groundbreaking book, *It's the Manager: Moving from Boss to Coach* it's worse than we thought. Traditional performance reviews and stack ratings are often so bad that they "make performance worse" one-third of the time, and only 22 percent of employees strongly agree that their pay and incentives motivate them to do what is best for their organization.[11] As Clifton and Harter state, "When employees are rewarded for putting themselves ahead of colleagues and customers, it fuels greed and dysfunctional competition." They also cite an often-told story used to discredit individual achievement-based incentives. In the 1990s Men's Wearhouse discovered one of its top-performing sales members was hogging sales. As an organization that valued individual success and achievement, an employee like this typically would be rewarded for such performance. However, Men's Wearhouse soon discovered that the practice had actually decreased morale among its other employees and was affecting its bottom line. How did it find out? After changing its incentive and reward program, its overall sales went up 30 percent—not just at that store, but across the company.[12]

With all we know and all the research we have from the past decade, it still shocks us that organizations feel compelled to instill complex rating and employee review systems. The aptly titled article "The Demise of the Annual Performance Review Has Been Greatly Exaggerated" reported that approximately 63 percent of employers still conduct annual performance reviews.[13] One of the most shocking companies to still use this archaic process is Amazon. For a company that did so much to change our entire business culture, it's astounding that it is one of the biggest champions of this outdated mode of performance management.

What's worse is that this is a new development. In 2021 Amazon announced it would from then on be aligning future compensation with annual reviews. Despite what executives have to say, Amazon employees have been vocal about what they view as a cutthroat culture, and they believe the new evaluation system "fanned the flames of office politics and stifled innovation." Amazon disputed claims that it uses a rank-and-yank system, but it did not respond to *Insider* reporters when they asked if Amazon had quotas for its performance-review ratings.

The Focus Has Been on the Wrong Group

We are not naive. We know there are truly low performers, employees whom absolutely need to be managed out of the organization. But our argument asks, "Why wait for the annual performance review to do so?" If you need to do it, you need to do it yesterday, because otherwise, not making the move costs you and your organization every day they aren't performing. Sure, forced rankings give managers an easy out to make those decisions, but it's too high a price to pay. And one of the biggest prices you're paying is the time and energy you're not spending on your most precious resource. And it's not the high performers. The ones who are really being harmed are the vast majority of employees who are being lumped in the middle and basically labeled as mediocre.

This is a huge area for improvement. Many companies are missing out on opportunities when they're preoccupied with only their high and low performers. If the bulk of your employee population is considered mediocre, then those employees are not getting the same kind of focus as top and low performers.

Organizations also overlook those who are only two or three years into their career. Typically, companies don't invest in them because they aren't part of their top 20 percent of high producers. You have very little time to make an impact on a new employee, and there is typically no return on investment in the first six to nine months while a new employee learns the job. By the time you break even, statistically, you have about nine months before that employee moves on. And if he or she does move on in the first eighteen months, your organization has already been operating at a loss for that one employee, and it will cost you 1.5 times the person's salary on average to be replaced, not to mention the loss of time.

Think of how many people like Mark Cuban, Steve Jobs, Walt Disney, and Thomas Edison are amid that group. Imagine if your managers got to know them; engage with them; harness their talents, skills, and potential; and align them with your organization's goals.

Even though bosses don't always know best, sometimes they do. For example, we only told you half of the story of Oprah Winfrey being "fired" for not being right for television news. She wasn't really fired at all. Rather, she was essentially promoted. What articles that list famous people who have been fired fail to mention is that her boss saw something else for Oprah, the bigger picture for his entire organization. Seeing that Oprah was too emotionally invested in the people affected by the news stories, the producer thought her empathetic nature might be better suited for a daytime talk show, and he created one for her—where, as we all know, she thrived. Imagine if organizations and their leaders worried less about compliance, ranking, and reviews, and more about the big picture, creating a culture of coaching and feedback that empowered employees to use their skills, talents, and natural gifts.

Why Has Everything Changed Except the Performance Review?

We always find it so interesting that the past hundred years have witnessed remarkable changes and shifts in how companies operate on every level—except when it comes to annual performance reviews. Yes, there have been small changes and shifts in directions, but for the most part it's the same. Meanwhile, technology has taken over almost every aspect of our working lives. As a result, every layer of an organization has adapted and changed its processes. There are no more typing pools, no phone switchboards.

Just think about how payroll was done one hundred, seventy, or forty years ago. Checks were handed out weekly. It's practically unheard of to receive a check today. (Some Gen Zers have never even seen a checkbook.)

Payroll is now completely automated. But it's not just payroll (and the process behind it) that's changed. You'd be hard-pressed to find a fax machine in an office building now. Even how we communicate and assign work is different. Everyone uses email, Slack, Zoom, texting, and a number of platforms to communicate and interact. People don't even have to be in the same country to work on projects together, let alone in the same office. Employees used to carry business cards and have massive Rolodexes on their desks to keep track of contacts, and now all workers have to do is log in to LinkedIn or Salesforce to reach out to leads and colleagues. There is no part of any organization that hasn't been dramatically transformed in the last fifty years, since Moore's Law accurately posited that the density of the microchip would double every two years. Now an iPhone is 8.6 million times more powerful than a mainframe computer was in 1964.

But despite all of these advances and changes, we still employ an antiquated employee evaluation process that started one hundred years ago. Though some may argue that they have changed their performance review, the change is in name only. What they mean to say is that they have moved the same process online. They ask the same questions and use the same metrics for evaluation.

Many years ago, in a previous role, Doug worked with a client to change its performance evaluation. In actuality, all this client did was digitize the process. When all was said and done, the online annual performance review was still the same long, twenty-two-page process.

Not long after the client finalized its digital evaluation form, it came to the United States to meet with one of its customers, Walmart. The client was stunned to discover that Walmart's evaluation form was just two pages long! The client immediately called Doug and was (rightfully) upset. "How could you let us build this stupid process of ours? Our people hate it. And we could have redesigned it and made it just two pages long!" It had forgotten that we had recommended it simplify the performance process, but at that time it was resistant to change. Moving a paper process to the digital world without rethinking or redefining the experience, and not considering the user experience, is a mistake far too many organizations make.

Key Takeaways

- The performance review is a relic of a bygone era that does not accord with the norms and realities of the modern workplace. It is harmful to the way we work today and to the people we work with.

- The way many companies operate, fostering talent and managing their workforce, in general, tends to be alienating and ineffective.
- Performance reviews lead companies to focus on the high and low performers at the expense of the broad swath of the workforce not in either category.
- Organizations are no longer hierarchical in the way they used to be, when the norm of annual reviews was established. It's time for a refresh.
- When feedback is subjective, and based solely on one person's opinion, most likely after only a few interactions, promotion becomes a question of which manager can argue best for their employees rather than which employees are best suited for a position, what growth potential they have, or if they are capable of taking on more.
- People don't always understand their roles or how they fit in the whole organization, which leads to disengagement.
- Don't wait for the annual performance review to evaluate and let go of poor performers.
- Organizations and their leaders should worry less about compliance, ranking, and reviews and more about the big picture, creating a culture of coaching and feedback that empowers employees to use their skills and talents to support the company's goals while also achieving their own.

CHAPTER 2

Make Work Better with Performance Enablement

Assurance, Trust, Shared Purpose, Teamwork

At the height of the Great Depression, Americans could not have been at a lower point. Many had survived the ravages of World War I only to see fascism spread like wildfire throughout Europe. They had survived a global pandemic that wiped out millions, and now those who survived couldn't even get a job, let alone bread to feed their families. Drought and famine ravaged the middle of the country. There was no president, no world leader, and no one person who could fix a free-falling economy alone. *There was no quick fix for any of it.* This would require a sea change—Americans had to reimagine themselves. Their leader knew it would require something beyond policy changes, new laws, or restructuring of government. What it required was something beyond all of this: empathy. Yes, the American people needed to know they were not alone, that there was "nothing to fear but fear itself."

Franklin D. Roosevelt didn't think it made much sense to wait for his annual State of the Union address to talk to the American people. It was unprecedented for sure, but unlike any other time in history, Roosevelt knew that the new technology (well, not so much new, but rather more widespread than ever) would allow for regular, consistent updates with the American people. His predecessor, Herbert Hoover, had used radio—but sporadically and only to shout orders and invectives. Conversely, Roosevelt instituted what he called his fireside chats to be a kind but controlled and steady voice for the nation. Over the course of his four terms as president, he gave thirty such chats. Through this technology, Roosevelt was able to talk directly with his fellow Americans—removing the previous barriers, both figurative and literal. He was no longer separated by a podium but was broadcast quite literally into their homes. He wasn't their superior, either; he was one of them and didn't speak down to his audience. He didn't oversimply or overcomplicate things with jargon or rhetoric. Roosevelt was just another American trying to make his way through the turbulent and confusing times; he just happened to be their elected leader.

He believed the best way to enact change was to establish a connection through open and honest (transparent) conversation. And in his mind, they were bidirectional conversations. He anticipated what his audience would be thinking and asking and responded in kind. For example, when he called everyone—man or woman—to join in the war effort from home, he anticipated resistance and responded in kind: "People should do their work as near their homes as possible. We cannot afford to transport a single worker into an area where there is already a worker available to do the job. In some communities, employers dislike to employ women. In others, they are reluctant to hire Negroes. In still others, older men are not wanted. We can no longer afford to indulge such prejudices or practices."[1] He knew what their objections would be and didn't wait to hear them.

But in many cases, he actually didn't have to anticipate much. After he started the fireside chats, he received hundreds of thousands of letters. Americans felt so comfortable with Roosevelt, many wrote to him expressing their fears, offering their suggestions and feedback, and even thanking him for restoring their confidence and trust in leadership, the banks, the war effort, or whatever topic he had addressed in the previous chat. People felt they were in a conversation with their leader and were answering his call to be part of the larger purpose. He needed their help to accomplish the impossible; he couldn't do it alone. His listeners felt that call and responded. And Roosevelt had a captive audience. The novelist Saul Bellow, remembering this time, wrote, "I can recall walking eastward on the Chicago Midway on a summer evening. . . . Drivers had pulled over, parking bumper to bumper, and turned on their radios to hear Roosevelt. . . . You could follow without missing a single word as you strolled by. You felt joined to these unknown drivers, men and women smoking their cigarettes in silence, not so much considering the president's words as affirming the rightness of his tone and taking assurance from it."[2]

Assurance

Citizens pulled their cars over and stopped what they were doing because when Roosevelt spoke to them, they felt seen, heard, understood—in a word, safe. With Roosevelt, there was no mincing words, no attempts to assuage a certain political affiliation. He asked for what was needed and respected his audience enough to respond in kind. By making himself a "vehicle for citizens' fears," as professor Jeremi Suri, author of *The Impossible Presidency: The Rise and Fall of America's Highest Office*, explains, he channeled those anxieties toward positive collective actions: depositing family savings back in banks, building

21

schools, planting trees, and engaging in many other 'make work' public activities."[3]

In other words, by employing empathy, Roosevelt was able to get a lot done. He was the vehicle, but empathy and the components of empathy—assurance, trust, teamwork, shared purpose—were his tires. With them, he could move mountains—or in this case, millions of hopeless, disengaged, and disenfranchised Americans—to have a unified sense of purpose. As Suri puts it so aptly, "Roosevelt did not act as a savior but as a public motivator for what Abraham Lincoln more than seventy years earlier had called the 'better angels of our nature.'"[4]

Roosevelt's fireside chats marked a complete divergence from his contemporaries. He was transparent in a way no leader had been up to that point. His chats were long and explained every part of his plan and process. Unlike his enemies—like Charles Lindbergh, who oversimplified arguments, removed nuance, and blamed others (Jewish people) for America's problems—Roosevelt chose to lay it all out, warts and all, and accept responsibility for America's issues, rather than place blame on any one party or group. This transparency and willingness to admit his own shortcomings engendered trust and a deep sense of connection. He gave audience members permission to look at things differently, accept responsibility, seek a deeper understanding, and have a shared sense of purpose.

Shared Sense of Purpose

Perhaps Roosevelt's most important accomplishment through the fireside chats was unify the American people, as Suri says, "by giving their painful experiences voice and by showing that he cared. His words sent a message to citizens that he had listened to them and that he was trying to feel what they felt. That is why so many Americans—hundreds of thousands—sent him letters after each speech. They believed he would continue to listen."[5]

Trust

Good leaders hear the needs of their employees, but great leaders *actively listen and care*. Great leaders don't have to have all the right answers. Roosevelt certainly didn't. As Suri points out, "Americans did not overcome economic depression and fascism because Roosevelt had the answers. He was deeply uncertain about what to do, and he had the wisdom not to pretend otherwise. Instead, Roosevelt empowered the people to help themselves, as one would expect in a democracy. The president provided citizens with motivation and the means to make collective improvements, working together. Teamwork produced public goods—from schools and roads to trees and art—not the other way around."[6]

Teamwork

Teamwork, as they say, makes the dream work. Roosevelt removed the hierarchy. Citizens didn't do what he told them to because he was their leader. That's not what motivated and empowered them to change. It was that they saw themselves as a part of something bigger than themselves.

As a democracy, America thrived by governing (collaborating)—both its leaders and its people—together. Roosevelt knew this. He knew to inspire a diverse populace to come together, he needed to show them first that he cared. As his cousin, the former US president, Theodore Roosevelt, had said, "Nobody cares how much you know until they know how much you care."

Today's Challenges

Like Roosevelt, leaders today, in organizations all over the world, are facing another uprising of fascism, political divides, economic instability, inflation, and a major war and crisis in Europe. In addition, today's leaders face climate change, a pandemic, the shift to hybrid and remote work, the Great Resignation, and so much more. In the nearly three decades Jamie has worked in HR and the performance management space, and in the nearly four decades Doug has worked as a leader and executive, we have never had a convergence of challenges like this. But rather than being novel challenges, these crises simply brought to the surface all the workplace problems that have existed for years. They didn't cause the problems; they *amplified* them. Everything seemed to wash ashore like one rogue wave: lack of diversity and inclusiveness, bias in its many forms, well-being, work-life balance versus integration, distrust, psychological safety, transparency, autonomy, agency, career development, poor support for managers, need for strategic alignment, generational differences, visibility across the organization, skills deficiencies, opacity of existing skill sets within companies, and the mismatch of skills and people to the work to be done. Only the wave isn't rogue. This is not a moment that will pass. No, these problems are here to stay and will continue to require solutions as we evolve and change as a workforce.[7]

As we see it, the crises are not problematic but rather an opportunity for real changes. Beyond the buzz phrases HR professionals love to use—for example, "the future of work," and "employee-first"—is now a truly unique convergence of business needs, strategic insight from HR, and workforce realities (working from home, hybrid models, AI, and so forth) that requires us to find ways to make work—finally—work for everyone. If leaders are truly determined to make work better for people, they too need to rethink and reimagine what their relationship as leaders, HR professionals, and employees is, and what it can be. They need to create cultures where assurance, trust, shared sense of purpose, teamwork, and collaboration can flourish, where leaders use transparency, communication, empathy, and whatever tools (technology and resources) are necessary to do so. To do that, to create a fresh approach to managing performance in a mutually beneficial way that enables everyone to do their best, the model should be the same four pillars of empathy that guided Roosevelt: *assurance, trust, teamwork, shared purpose.*

How do we create a system based on those four pillars that works for all our stakeholders? We begin by listening.

Stakeholders, Tell Me What You Want, What You Really, Really Want

While most performance-management programs encourage enabling performance, strategic alignment, and business agility, the only way to ensure that these actually take place is if the people tasked to do so find their work meaningful and feel valued, engaged, and accomplished. All the stakeholders in an organization—business leaders (executives), HR professionals, managers, or employees—must feel that their needs are being met. We asked each of these people to, in the immortal words of the Spice Girls, "Tell us what you want, what you really, really, really want." What we have found out in our work with top companies follows.[8]

25

Employees Want Empathy (Assurance, Trust, Shared Sense of Purpose, Teamwork/Connection), Guidance, Recognition, and to Know the Work They Do Matters

Employees want to know that managers and coworkers have their backs and can support them in accomplishing their work. They need guidance to break through barriers and challenges, and to prioritize and reprioritize activities as business requirements shift, so that they can focus on what really matters. Employees want to be recognized and fairly rewarded for their efforts. They expect managers to understand and support their aspirations, providing opportunities and tools for ongoing development. All this, of course, happens under the umbrella of relationships, connection, and trust—that is, empathy. Above all, employees want to see how their contributions matter.

HR Leaders Want Support, Strategic Alignment with Their Leaders, and Useful Data

To support their leaders' desires to know what's happening in a company, HR professionals want to be more efficient so that they can focus on high-value strategic initiatives rather than administrative tasks and processes. They also need to know what their executive leadership team's goals are. Jamie recalls when she was working with a global manufacturing organization just before Christmas break. She went into her CEO's office and asked, "I really need you to establish some goals for the month ahead, because I need to make them visible for our employees." Jamie was met with, "Yeah, yeah, yeah. I have stuff to do before I leave for the holiday. I will get back to you in the middle of January." Jamie, feeling mischievous, asked, "So you're telling me that there are eighty thousand employees in your organization who you don't necessarily think it's important to let know what you want them to focus on over the next month?" She made her point, and he posted his goals.

Likewise, many HR leaders want to leverage employee data, compiled across the organization, to tell a story. They want to translate the information meaningfully to both leaders and employees. Serving as a conduit between the employees, managers, and executives, HR professionals help everyone see what's going on in an organization and help each feel valued or have a shared sense of purpose. They require data to see if employees are meeting with their managers, if goals are being discussed, where employees are with strategic initiatives, and if their goals align with the strategic goals of the business. If leaders want to know what's going on with employees—why there is high turnover, for example—HR workers want to communicate their employees' level of job satisfaction.

Managers Want Coaching and Support Tools

Managers want frameworks, practical tools, and guidance so that they can be effective team leaders, especially with the complexities of hybrid and remote work. Their roles are shifting from managing to coaching, requiring a new set of skills to enable their direct reports to achieve their work goals and development aspirations and to feel like valued members of the team. With so much attention on the influence that managers have on employee retention, managers want tools to help them foster connection, improve collaboration, and promote employee development.

Executives Need to Know What Their Employees' and Teams' Goals Are, What They're Doing, Where They're Going, and What Their Needs Are

Business leaders need to see what's happening with workforce productivity and hear their own employees' views about the company. As Betterworks advisory board member and HR analyst Josh Bersin puts it, "If you're the CEO of a big pharmaceutical company, or Sundar Pichai at Google, and there are 175,000 employees, you see the costs going up but the revenue not going up as fast. You're going to think, *How come we're falling behind?* What he wants is visibility. He wants to know where they are behind—which departments, groups, products, geographies. . . . He wants to know why so he can put his attention on those areas."[9]

That is to say that leaders need to have their finger on the pulse of what's going on in the deepest veins and arteries of the heart of their companies. They have to know what is going in and what is going out, what's making it pump, and what's the electrical current—that is, the vibe. They want to be forewarned of any obstacles and obstructions. What can they do to optimize performance? If they can't see, hear, or know what's going on in the lifeblood of their organization—their people—they can't plan, forecast, respond, or lead.

Performance Enablement Makes Work Better[10]

To give these stakeholders what they need, we must evolve performance management into performance enablement. Traditional performance management is broken and almost universally despised, a point Josh Bersin makes clear in his book *Irresistible: The Seven Secrets of the World's Most Enduring, Employee-Focused Organizations.* He shares a story of a large company that spent $1 million annually on performance management, had a nine-step calibration process, and devoted nearly the entire month of December on performance reviews. However, when the company surveyed employees to learn what single activity they'd shed, the number one answer was, overwhelmingly, "performance management."

The seventy-plus-year-old process that was designed as a competitive assessment to rank employees and weed out nonperformers is not working, and it won't ever work. Yet many organizations continue to try to tweak it rather than start all over and rethink it. Sure, many organizations have been evolving to more of a coaching and development model, but the transformation is incomplete and must evolve further in light of employees' new needs and expectations.

Bersin says, "People are tired and burned out; 81% say they're overworked. Now the leader of one of the largest companies says productivity has to improve. There's a big disconnect between what executives believe their employees should do and what employees are feeling." Bersin argues that that is a "design" problem. "You can't just give people more money and think that's going to solve it," he says. "What we need is a new operating system."

A New Operating System: Performance Enablement

What is the right answer? With so many working under a hybrid model or remotely, communication with managers and teammates is tougher, meaning people's signals get misaligned. It's more difficult for employees or teams to keep their goals aligned with the strategic goals of the organization in a complex environment. In an era of continual business disruption, business strategies are always subject to change, in turn requiring employees to readjust what they're working on. And, of course, relationships can become more easily strained when the workforce is distributed and virtual and more is asked of them or expected of them.

In such an environment, managers, teams, and individual contributors have to find ways to clearly communicate, stay on track, maintain the culture, and support and cheer each other on. And they expect to be able to do this easily and with minimal friction. This means that conversations, constructive feedback, guidance, alignment and realignment, and connections have to happen in the flow of work—in the applications people use every day. What's more, these processes must be fair and promote individuals' aspirations. They should encourage BHAGs (big, hairy, audacious goals) and innovation and be data-driven and continuous. Essentially, we're talking about an integrated solution that puts more of the responsibility for performance in the hands of employees in an empowering way that becomes an everyday habit.

And we advocate for making those BHAGs public and being open about where a company is going, what it wants to achieve, and where the collective ambitions of its employees are pointing. Secrecy is not always the way forward; openness in certain things has great benefits. Openness not only allows employees to feel included in the overall mission of an organization but also makes possible their valuable input into what those goals could be.

Ask Not What You Can Do for Your Company, but What Your Company Can Do for You

Employment is not a one-way street. In the modern workplace, where employees have options and working for a company until retirement is rare, the question "What are you doing for the company?" is not the only one to ask. Another question is "What is the company doing for you?" In other words, for a workforce that craves meaning in and recognition for their work, employees need to see how they are contributing to the whole. Therefore, yet another vital question is "Who do you want to be inside the organization?" By prioritizing the mutual exchange of value and helping employees see how investing their time and talents in the company will help them further their longer-term career goals, the conversation between the employee and the managers becomes "How can I help you get there?" This means that employees and their managers work together to come up with one or two developmental goals to give employees the skills they need, and the continuous feedback required, to ensure they reach that level. That feedback can be scheduled or ad hoc—and it's available for everyone.

Too often, employees don't hear the feedback necessary to help them redirect course or get ahead of a problem before it escalates. To cultivate high-performing teams and a strong internal pipeline of talent, leaders need to be serious about creating a culture of feedback.

Cisco called this practice "fast failure." Employees can fail, receive the feedback they need to recover quickly, and then move forward. That feedback can't wait for a midyear or year-end review cycle to have an impact. The most innovative and successful companies that have adopted fast failure also have a stretch mentality—workers there aren't afraid to get uncomfortable, fail quickly, and push themselves to find solutions. Those companies are just as quick to give recognition to those who deserve it as they are to give criticism.

Together, these powerful, proven elements of manager support, feedback, and employee engagement represented a seismic shift in the way companies think about managing performance. And this shift was so different, in fact, that calling it "management" didn't really make sense. Thus, *performance enablement* was born.

Defined, a *modern performance enablement solution* is one that moves away from the outdated concepts of hierarchy and control, adopting instead a framework that places employees' needs at the center. It gives employees the opportunity to create meaningful developmental and performance goals that align with their company's strategic goals and equips managers to frequently coach and enable employees—rather than dictate and evaluate. Performance enablement provides managers with the tools and resources they need to lead and instills confidence in employees that they'll receive the support they need. This leads to a virtuous cycle of better business results and employees who are more satisfied, productive, and engaged. In short, it's everything the traditional approach to performance management fails to be.

How do you know if your approach to performance is helping or hindering? Besides the obvious indicators—the success and growth of your business—performance-enabled organizations share a few distinct characteristics:

- They're forward-looking, not backward-looking: Teams take a proactive approach to problem-solving, and reflection is used to inform future strategies (not place blame).
- Evaluations are not punitive: Managers focus on coaching and take ownership of enabling employees to close the gap between current and target performance.
- Conversations and feedback are part of the company culture and the way work gets done—they do not rely solely on annual or biannual reviews.
- They value human connection and relationships, and their company culture is marked by high degrees of trust and respect.

- HR leaders use data and insights to help managers understand the complete employee picture and make concerted efforts to reduce bias and build trust.

- They see the important connection between learning and development and performance, and the organizations integrate their L&D or learning-experience platform into the performance process to drive adoption.

- Their employee digital experience is designed with the end user in mind and not the convenience of the administrators. They understand that inelegant, good-enough software might check a box, but it rarely adds value or drives transformation.

A Case Against Cascading Goals

One of the best things that has come from these practices—making BHAGs public and adopting performance enablement—is that they eliminate what's known as *cascading goals*, a practice where goals for teams and individuals would be determined by the leader. When a CEO passes goals down to top leadership, and then those leaders tell those below them what their goals should be, most employees can't connect to that. We know feeling engaged with one's work and having a sense of meaning in what one does are essential to long-term satisfaction, which is why we've found that it works best when employees are empowered to create goals that align their role and the work they do to the company's goals. When employees create and align their own goals, they feel more engaged and connected to them because, as we all know, people are more likely to support what they help create. Seeing a direct connection between their work and its impact on the company is a surefire way to ensure that employees feel valued and believe that their work matters.

We see that all the time with leaders and organizations that use our software. Top leaders meet and reflect at the end of each quarter. *What were our company goals for the last quarter? How did we do against those?* They celebrate achievements and identify challenges. They make all of this information visible, and instead of dictating what everyone else has to do, managers meets with their reports and say, "Here are our company's goals for the quarters. Some things have adjusted. Now, how do your goals fit in?"

The employee determines the goals, coming up with the three to five most important things they're going to do this quarter to help the company achieve its goals, along with one or two personal goals to grow their career in the company. Then, together with their manager, the employee determines which ones are aspirational (not likely to be fully achieved but something to shoot for) and which ones can be 100 percent attained.

But the conversation covers more than just achieving the company's goals. Creating a dialogue forces management to say, "How are you? What do you want to be in the organization? How can I help you get there? What are the skills you need to have, or what development needs can we help you with? Maybe there are a couple of classes you can take. Or is there someone we can team you with to shadow? Do you need a coach?" The value of these goal conversations is greater than the goal-setting itself because now the managers are invested in the career of that person inside the organization. The value of the process is greater than the task.

Instead of giving feedback, we want people to start thinking about giving *feed-forward*—meaning instead of only looking backward, they look forward to what employees can do to move themselves and their companies to the next level.

Feed-forward also serves the leaders too, because it forces leadership to look at goals for the whole organization, not just to top company goals. By looking at what's happened at the individual level, they can see what goals are bubbling up from below in the organization. Individuals can have some lofty goals or innovative ideas the leaders hadn't thought of. Now, this may feel like a lot of pressure on managers. Instead of giving feedback once a year in annual performance reviews, they're now being asked to do it more frequently (we recommend at least quarterly).

That change should be modeled from the top too. One tool we strongly recommend using—which we use ourselves—is quarterly reflections. Ideally, leaders share their goals with their employees in reflections at least on a quarterly basis. At the end of each quarter, the leader could say, "Here's where we are, what we did, what we didn't do, and why, and here are the obstacles we faced. Here's what we plan on doing differently, and here are new goals." When leaders set goals, that empowers and guides everyone in an organization to align their own goals to those of the company. We've found that simply doing these reflections leads to engagement and increased confidence in leadership. Employees see the leadership setting goals on a regular basis, and they see their part in accomplishing these goals—in other words, they feel they matter and are making an impact.

We have found that usually after about a year HR begins to realize that with these frequent engagements, an annual performance review to assess salary or compensation is not needed. Why? Because they will be able to give compensation increases when people deserve them—no matter what time of year.

The University of Phoenix Gives Its
Performance Management a Fix

The University of Phoenix employs more than 3,100 people and has been an accredited higher-education institution for the past forty years. In 2017 it underwent a substantial transition when its publicly traded parent company was sold to a private equity firm. With this transition came a new president and a directive to reevaluate the organization's values and employer culture.

At the core, the university wanted to improve its honesty and transparency. One way the president did this was by removing the annual performance review. According to Jeff Andes, who joined the University of Phoenix in 2013 and is now vice president of talent management there, "The employer's culture had drifted far from the organization's entrepreneurial origins in innovation, becoming very corporate."[11] As a seasoned HR professional, Andes was more than happy to do away with the traditional annual performance review too. Andes helped champion this and other fundamental changes to reshape the organizational culture, and he gathered information. Data from surveys showed that employees perceived a lack of transparency within management. As a result, the University of Phoenix set about strengthening the value of honesty at its forefront.

But even before the new leaders changed the way work processes functioned, they knew they had to make structural changes to the environment, to make it clear to the employees that they were serious about a culture of transparency and continuous communication. They remodeled their offices, so that managers and executives had windows, to break down walls and give more visibility. Blinds were removed from conference rooms. They also eliminated their private elevator bank for the C-suite at the headquarters. In addition, the University of Phoenix thought the figurative, not just structural, barriers between managers and employees needed to come down. Like so many companies struggling with doing away with hierarchies, the University of Phoenix found itself working to change mindsets as well.

Organizations are no longer hierarchical in the way they were when the norm of annual reviews was established. These days, many employees work more frequently with people outside their own teams, and even their own companies, than they do with their managers, so a single annual assessment by the manager couldn't possibly capture the employee's total performance and all their interactions. When feedback is subjective and based solely on one person's opinion, most likely after only a few interactions, it becomes a question of which manager can argue best for their employees, rather than which employee is best suited for a position, what growth potential the person has, or if the worker is capable of taking on more. For the better assessment to occur, managers need to have regular, meaningful conversations with their employees.

Of course, these meaningful conversations are critical to employee engagement, which has become a real challenge for many organizations, especially since the hierarchies have shifted. People don't always understand their roles or how they fit in the whole organization, and it's leading to disengagement (with 85 percent of workers reporting they are disengaged at work and 74 percent looking for a new job).[12] With nearly 70 percent of people in companies not understanding how their work contributes to the goals of the entire organization, it's costing the US economy up to $605 billion a year.[13] (Disengaged employees are likely to make more than 60 percent more mistakes than engaged employees. Engaged employees are more likely to show up for work.)[14] But without transparency, it's impossible to see the big picture and how this disengagement is affecting the whole.

By replacing the conventional, compliance-minded performance review, with the focus of rating employees and meeting company quotas, the University of Phoenix removed a barrier that kept managers from continually checking in with their employees. Instead of waiting all year to talk to employees, they were now able to communicate with employees on a continual basis via frequent manager-employee interactions, through what they called the Everyday Performance Development Program. They designed it to better support both employees and managers. What they found after a year of the program was that employees began to report greater satisfaction with their jobs and increased their productivity. They were also less likely to quit or look elsewhere for work. Andes said one of the aims of the new program was to foster engagement on an ongoing basis and in the moment when it needed to happen, rather than waiting a year when the moment has long since passed. In addition, they opted for less formal quarterly check-ins.[15] Andes adds, "We wanted it to be short and quick, because you're doing it so often. For us, a continuous two-way conversation is also one in which employees and managers are thinking more deeply about their responses because they feel more invested and are following up on what they heard with positive action."[16]

University managers implemented the program by aiming for two or three questions per quarter, and they didn't want to do anything with any hint of the "old way" of doing things—that is, paperwork, or what they called "forced documentation." They believed lack of paperwork would facilitate a more relaxed and conversational experience for both the manager and employee—the emphasis being on the relationship.

Relationships matter, and at its heart, the performance-review model of employee assessment is adversarial and an anathema to a good relationship. It is a means for seeking out faults that are all too likely to be dealt with in a punitive fashion; even when the performance review is conducted in an ideal fashion, an employee is likely to take umbrage at the process. The example of the University of Phoenix is an instructive one, and lessons are to be learned for leaders and managers who stand to benefit from adopting similar tactics for their own organizations. This concern is at the heart of what we have to offer here.

Key Takeaways

- What people want most from their leadership are assurance, trust, teamwork, and a shared sense of purpose.
- Performance enablement is a new and far better path toward organizational effectiveness and employee satisfaction than old-fashioned performance management.
- When goals are rigid and don't reflect changing work circumstances, employees feel trapped, and goals are viewed as meaningless.
- Employee goals should be agile and tied to the company's top-level goals and should cover personal development and help employees strive to do more with their careers.
- Employment is not a one-way street. In the modern workplace, where employees have options and it's rare that someone stays at a company until retirement, the question "What are you doing for the company?" is not the only one to ask. Also important is "What is the company doing for you?"

- Organizations, and people within them, should be open about what their goals are, to maximize employee inclusion and encourage invaluable input from the workers.
- The example of the University of Phoenix shows how these measures, when implemented, can result in a thriving organization that makes performance enablement a way to inform both employees' performances and the goals of the company.
- One should forget cascading goals. And instead of giving feedback, we want people to start thinking about giving feed-forward—meaning instead of only looking backward, they look forward to what employees can do to move themselves and their companies to the next level.

CHAPTER 3

Performance Enablement from the Ground Up

A Continuous Approach to Connection and Engagement

When something is continuous, it's not necessarily *constant*—but it's also not limited to arbitrary points most often dictated by the calendar. At most companies today, performance discussions happen at predefined intervals, usually at the end of a half or full fiscal year—meaning that the feedback and recognition associated with important project deliverables, client wins, or product launches may be completely ineffective or outdated by the time it's delivered some months later. It's certainly out of context when it is.

In a performance-enabled organization, however, conversations and feedback are embedded into the way work gets done. Frequent, lightweight conversations that don't require exhaustive preparation from either managers or employees and that focus on personal- and career-development goals and work product ensure that employees are engaged and feel supported.

Furthermore, the periodic nature of traditional performance processes could actually be holding one back from achieving desired outcomes. In today's world, companies have no option but to be agile, adapting to constant and rapid changes in the marketplace. Agile companies have a people-centered culture that features rapid learning and fast decision cycles enabled by technology and guided by a powerful common purpose to cocreate value for all stakeholders. Such agile operating models allow for quick and efficient reconfigurations of strategy, structure, processes, people, and technology toward value-creating and value-protecting opportunities.

Obviously, yearlong goals are very likely to go out of date in a system that doesn't allow for a shift in priorities—or a process that doesn't encourage active tracking of those priorities. Similarly, infrequent conversations between managers and employees mean responding to new information or learning new skills to cater to new needs or building trust and internal commitment around revised strategies don't happen effectively. When these things are missing, not only does individual performance suffer, but overall company performance does too.

A Scalable Enterprise Platform

Businesses of today are complex. They are increasingly global in nature and, as a result, need to deal with varying local labor laws, legislative-compliance needs, and reporting requirements. Many are structurally complex, with multiple divisions, subsidiaries, and joint ventures. They use myriad technology systems that need to work with each other. Top companies need to attract, retain, and grow their global talent base and have to invest in a number of employee-centric practices, such as accessibility and inclusion, across their enterprise. Effective performance technology needs to support a dynamic workforce and workplace, incorporate accessibility as a core design principle, comply with local and international regulations, integrate with existing and future investments, and keep data safe.

Interconnected and Integrated

At Betterworks, we use aggregated data from our customers' use of our platform to help us better understand the impact we have. One thing that this data has taught us is that the various aspects of performance management are highly interconnected—and ultimately, the sum of the parts can make a significant impact. Consider these findings:

- Customers that have conversations and check-ins see an increase in goal progress by 24 percent.
- Customers who use feedback see an increase in goal progress by 15 percent.
- Customers who use recognition see an increase in goal progress of 10 percent.
- Programs that effectively utilize goals, conversations, feedback, and recognition (versus goal-setting alone) see an average increase in goal progress by 30 percent.

The various modules in Betterworks's performance-enablement solution are highly interconnected. When an employee is having a conversation with their manager, their goals, training-course progress, and feedback and recognition they've received are all front and center so they can have focused, productive, and timely discussions. These practices reinforce one another and, together, create the habits, relationships, and collaboration that drive great performance.

We've discussed at the highest level what the key components of modern performance enablement are and what differentiates performance management and performance enablement. We have gone into some detail about the benefits of performance enablement and the sea change that organizations have witnessed as a result of adopting this new and better approach. Now, we'll dive into each of the capabilities essential for enabling great performance at all levels of an organization.

Conversations: Prioritizing and Enabling Employee Success

We believe in promoting what we call purpose-driven and impactful discussions between managers and their direct reports. This kind of trust-building and open, honest communication with managers is essential—after all, we know that a majority of employees don't quit companies; they quit managers. In fact, Gallup found that employees crave authentic relationships with their managers—they want to be able to talk about both work and life and connect on a human-to-human level. With collective visibility into employee goals, progress, feedback, and engagement, managers and employees have a holistic view of all the information needed for valuable and productive conversations. The result? Higher trust and stronger relationships promote alignment and unlock opportunities.

Of the five generations in the workforce today, Generations X, Y, and Z especially don't want to be talked to once a year about their performance; they want to be talked to on a regular basis. As people who are accustomed to a flexible world of work, they can—and expect to—adapt to new ideas and projects regularly and want the opportunity to collaborate and get feedback. And while this may seem daunting to new managers or busy leaders with several direct reports, Betterworks has developed several expertly designed templates to support a variety of conversation types to reduce the burden:

- Goal-setting
- Two-way feedback
- Progress updates

- Performance
- Career development

Fundamentally, the best conversations should be balanced—that is, they should be bidirectional. Most organizations think that development conversations are top-down and backward-looking—managers evaluate employees by reviewing work from the last quarter. If conversations are held regularly, there is no need to look backward. They should be present- and future-focused and invite the opportunity for employees to provide managers with feedback as well. This two-way feedback loop creates more balanced opportunities, which in turn increases operational excellence for the entire company.

Prompt, Meaningful, Customized, and Visible Feedback and Recognition

We've found that the best conversations include feedback from a variety of stakeholders, including managers and peers from cross-functional teams. The variety helps reinforce positive behaviors, build employee confidence, enable employees to develop new capacities, and strengthen collaboration.

Although employee feedback is the key driver of modern performance management, most people think feedback is either positive or negative. But that is usually what describes a manager's and an employee's emotional reactions to feedback, not the feedback itself.

Managers may assume that employees don't want feedback they perceive as negative. But employees crave feedback that can help them understand and improve their work. According to a survey conducted by Price Waterhouse Coopers (PwC), nearly 60 percent of employees said they would like to see feedback on a daily or weekly basis, and that number is 72 percent for employees under the age of thirty (Gen Z). More than 75 percent believe the feedback is valuable and helpful to do their jobs, but only about 30 percent of employees said they actually receive it.[1] This is interesting, since we know that 69 percent of employees would work harder if they felt their efforts were recognized. As long as critical feedback is framed appropriately and doesn't dwell on mistakes, employees typically won't shut down or react negatively to it.

We think feedback falls into four specific categories:

- *Directive feedback* proposes specific actions for the team member to take to improve their performance; essentially, it tells the recipient what to do or how to do it. Here's an example: "Add more dynamic images to your PowerPoint slides to make them more engaging."

- *Contingency feedback* offers an evaluation or consequence based on a specific action. It may praise actions taken or suggest a new course of action to change an outcome. For example, "If you continue to talk over people in meetings, they will be less apt to collaborate with you."

- *Attribution feedback* deals with qualities, and it may assign a label to the employee. For example, "You're productive."

- *Impact feedback* focuses on the outcomes of the employee's actions on their team members and colleagues, prompting people to evaluate their own performance. Here's typical impact feedback: "Because of your planning and creative thinking, the customer event was popular and a major success."

Of these, impact feedback tends to be most effective because it explains why the employee's actions matter, helping the person act more thoughtfully or strategically in the future.

Empathetic Conversations That Help Deliver Constructive Criticism

Of course, when offering constructive criticism, we believe empathy needs to be the main driver of the conversation. Seek to understand the other person's feelings. Assume positive intent. The ideal feedback session focuses on obstacles the employee is facing, skills they may be lacking and in need of coaching, and possibly other issues. Don't assume that mistakes are the result of ill will or laziness. We've found that when you let the employee know that you understand why he or she took a course of action, you are more than likely to get an accurate assessment of the situation as well as find solutions to ameliorate it. If you don't understand where the worker is coming from, ask and try to understand the thought process.

We've also found that feedback, to be most effective, should be both *lightweight* and *continuous,* which is a fancy way of saying that it should be ongoing and not exhaustive. The most effective feedback is clear, concise, and to the point. The feedback should be future-pointed: "I want to address this now so that we can help you in the future." And the best feedback happens in the moment it's required—when the action has occurred. Waiting a year is far too late.

For managers, feedback should be easy to contextualize, customize, and give. We know that employee feedback is not one-size-fits-all. Department, function, role, and hierarchy impact the type of feedback needed to improve performance and cultivate growth. Feedback can vary in cadence and type. It may be scheduled quarterly or ad hoc.

We believe a best practice is to encourage employees to give and receive feedback among their peers and cross-functional project teams, not solely among the managers in their reporting structure. Frequent, relevant feedback coupled with *personal recognition* have the power to transform employee performance and culture. Recognition promotes teamwork, collaboration, and cultural values—and you can amplify that impact by making appreciation visible company-wide.

Case Study: CBORD Working to Create Dream Conversations

One of our clients, CBORD, was looking for a complete talent-management solution to attract the best people, drive engagement throughout a widely distributed organization, and spur peak performance in an accountable way. The company insisted on a nonhierarchical, two-way conversation between its employees and managers that allowed for continuous and open communication, feedback, and training.

CBORD is the world's leading provider of integrated technology solutions powering housing, access, food service, nutrition, e-commerce, and card systems for K–12 and higher education, acute care, senior living, and business campuses. CBORD's products and services are used by more than seven thousand organizations in the United States, Canada, South Africa, Australia, New Zealand, and the Middle East.

CBORD's main challenge was that it wanted an engagement and performance management platform to guide employees' entire career lifecycle through what CBORD's Human Resources Vice President Katherine Creek calls "the sum of our values, beliefs, interactions, and behaviors with each other and our clients." CBORD expresses those values in the acronym DREAM, which stands for "dynamic, restless, empowered, accountable, and mindful."[2]

The company has DREAM goals instead of OKRs (objectives and key results), DREAM checks for conversations, and DREAM feedback for feedback sessions, and it calls recognitions DREAM shouts. CBORD managers assess how employees live out DREAM values as they do their jobs, and when a manager or a peer awards recognitions in DREAM shouts, each is assigned a hashtag with one of the DREAM values.

CBORD insists on frequent DREAM conversations but prefers they be driven by employees, not managers. "When our team members are empowered and well-informed, they understand clearly where their performance is and what their managers' expectations are, and the team members hold the managers accountable for developing employees. Team members are encouraged to develop their own voice, which makes them more loyal and more empowered to get more done," says Creek. Employees understand clearly how their work helps CBORD move toward its strategic goals, which is hard to come by in the modern workplace.[3]

After implementing Betterworks's app, performance development became a strength of CBORD. In its annual engagement survey, CBORD saw increases in both participation and engagement scores compared to the previous year. By building a more engaged workforce, productivity and business success have followed.[4]

Creating a Culture of Readiness That Focuses on Constructive Feedback

When clients ask us to help them with their performance management, we see repeatedly that while they want to change—that is, they want a company that encourages feedback, both structured and unstructured—many companies can't do so without their culture changing. This means moving away from a closed culture with no transparency and therefore no trust that employees can handle information and trust that the leaders know what they are doing. These companies want to provide feedback, but many simply have no idea how to.

Cultures that switch to giving continuous feedback—in the moment and during regular reviews—will find it difficult if trust for the system isn't in place. Employees accustomed to performance reviews or a rank-and-yank evaluation system are going to prepare themselves much differently than those accustomed to regular check-ins. Those only used to annual feedback sessions may find regular formal and even informal check-ins intrusive or even like an attack in which they have to defend themselves or their performance out of fear of losing their jobs or not getting a hoped-for promotion.

This is why training is so important. Giving and receiving feedback is much more nuanced and complicated than simply rating an employee or asking the employee how he or she is measuring up to goals.

We think that creating a culture of feedback starts at the top. If the leaders in the company aren't willing to accept feedback, own their mistakes, and be transparent about their own and the company's goals, how then can they expect their employees to do so? Employees need assurance that they are safe to give and receive feedback without fear of retaliation. They need to be able to fail, fail quickly, and be afforded the tools to recover, change, and improve. The companies that are the most successful at encouraging feedback, and getting the right kind, are those that invest in coaching both employees and managers on how to do so. The coaching involves being more empathetic.

Intuit Creates Strategic Alignment and Strong Relationships with a Goal Framework[5]

Intuit is a global technology platform that develops and sells financial, accounting, and tax-preparation software and related services for small businesses, accountants, the self-employed, and individuals. The company, headquartered in Mountain View, California, employs about ninety-five hundred employees. Intuit's products include the tax-preparation application TurboTax, the personal-finance app Mint, and the small business accounting program QuickBooks. At Intuit, performance management is a core business process that supports the company's mission and vision. "At the core of Intuit's performance management philosophy is our mission to deliver great products and services to our customers. We know that will fuel success for the organization," said Humera Shahid, vice president of talent development at Intuit.

The foundation for Intuit's performance-management process is a strategic goal-setting framework driven by top leadership. A few years ago, the leadership team decided to position the organization as a platform company—with different brands under a single unifying platform. Goal-setting from the very top became the vehicle to create alignment. "When we talk about goal-setting, it's really a business-driven process," Humera said.

The goal-setting framework is published and transparent for all employees to align with. It starts with the company mission: to power prosperity around the world, accomplished by being an AI-driven platform. And it does so by supporting what the company calls big bets, such as strategic company goals and long-term initiatives for customer products and services.

"Our big bets include things like how we help our customers have more financial predictability, how we help them run their business, and how we put money in the pockets of our consumers," explained Humera. Intuit has developed what it calls input goals, similar in principle to OKRs, to ensure the success of each big bet. These goals answer questions such as the following:

- What will you do?
- How will you be successful?
- How will we measure success?

Intuit's senior leadership team decides on company input goals annually; the team then discusses goal progress at monthly meetings to check in and collaborate further. Intuit's employees also set individual input goals around similar questions:

- How do I support given my role?
- What does success look like?
- How can I measure success?

Additionally, employees are expected to set development goals to ensure they can grow their skills and careers at Intuit. Individuals also review goal progress with their managers on a monthly basis, at which time goals can be fine-tuned or changed if needed.

The pandemic hit small businesses particularly hard, and Intuit had to adapt to support its customers. For instance, the change in the 2019 tax deadline had many repercussions for Intuit. The company's agile goal-setting approach was well suited to enable the flexibility required to quickly recalibrate. The monthly check-ins for goals also helped Intuit managers understand what employees could realistically accomplish with the changed work conditions brought about by the pandemic, such as changes in their childcare responsibilities.

Goal-achievement levels are set as challenging, and the expectation is that most goals will be accomplished at 75 percent. "If we are achieving 100 percent on all goals, it means we are not challenging ourselves enough," said Humera.

Goals are transparent across the organization; an employee can see the goals of any other employee. This transparency is part of the organization's culture and helps drive collaboration and effective discussions to get the best outcomes for customers.

Goal-setting has grown to close to 100 percent adoption, because it is driven by senior leadership. It is not viewed as an HR administrative task, and it has proven to build alignment with the company's mission and vision. Employees ask for the company goals, to help set the stage for their goals every year. "They want to know that we're all working towards the same shared objectives for the company together. That's the power of goal alignment and goal-setting from the very top," said Humera.

The monthly feedback and goal-discussion process is also easier to do because of the embedded templates. These give individuals an agenda for their check-ins and provide managers with key insights into what goals are progressing well and where employees might need help. Most employees and managers find the performance-management approach useful, but there is always room for improvement. As a next step, Humera and her team plan to connect their learning-management system so people can get automatic learning suggestions based on their development goals. Additionally, the team wants to double down on longer-term career aspirations. "What's most important to us is that our employees and managers have a really strong relationship. Any tools we put in place enable transparency, accountability, and development."

Whereas the tools are important, so too is the culture. In fact, one can have all the tools in the world at one's disposal, but without a culture that focuses on feedback, it's nearly impossible to sustain transparency, accountability, and development.

Google: A Look at How to Give Empathetic Feedback to Create a Change Management Culture of Readiness

One of the best examples of an organization that has a process in place for giving feedback is Google. We admire Google's process, most especially how Google provides extensive training to managers and details explicitly how it should be done and has even published its re:Work new manager training facilitator guide. The company knows that giving feedback is uncomfortable, but it has an antidote. Google calls it *positive intent*. When managers and leaders are clear about their intention and their role and come from a place of "positive intent"—that is, wanting someone to improve, succeed, and meet the employee's or the company's goals—they will have better outcomes.

Google asks its managers to ask themselves several questions before giving feedback, to test to see if the feedback is coming from a place of positive intent:

- Why do you want to deliver this feedback, and how do you intend to do it?
- Do you intend to help your direct report have a better career and experience here?

- Do you intend to give the feedback in a way that minimizes their sense of discomfort but also gets the point across?
- Can I deliver this message with genuine empathy for their perspective?[6]

Google has a protocol it calls SBI, which stands for Situation, Behavior, Impact, that is helpful when giving feedback:

- Situation you want to discuss
- Behavior in the situation
- Impact of that behavior

To understand the situation better, Google recommends that managers find the root cause of the needed feedback:

- Is it a lack of skill, a lack of information, obstacles, or a lack of will?
- Were the expectations clear from the outset?

So many issues in life, not just in work, are a result of unmet expectations. Often, we think we've been very clear with what we're asking, but our message wasn't heard or received.

Once you've established common ground and have a clear understanding of the situation, behavior, and impact, in addition to the expectations, it's time to deliver the constructive or developmental feedback. We believe it's best to do so using empathy—the *assurance* that you're giving the feedback with a positive intent so that the recipient can *trust* you're on the same *team* and have a *shared sense of purpose* (meeting the individual's goals and that of the team's or organization's).

When you're coming from a place of empathy and understanding, with a positive intent, it helps, Google recommends, if you have consistent criteria on which you're evaluating the employee. Google's managerial feedback tracking recommends asking yourself the following:

- Have you outlined expectations and anticipated outcomes for your direct report?
- Have you defined criteria for success for each person on the team?
- As you judge the direct report's performance or interpersonal skills, think about how you would evaluate that behavior if it came from a different person—for example, someone of a different gender or social group. Are you evaluating the person consistently?
- If the direct report was female, would her action have been typically seen as fine if the employee were male? (For example, if the person said, "I completely disagree with this direction," would you consider that aggressive if a woman said it but assertive if a man said it?)[7]

Of course, all of this is easier said than done and requires that managers and leaders are mindful of their biases. Everyone is biased. Everyone has life experiences and work experiences, along with socioeconomic, cultural, religious, political, gender, and knowledge-based biases. Part of delivering feedback is filtering it in a way so you become aware your feedback is not based on assumptions. Google recommends asking these questions:

- Do I filter what I say based on assumptions, and can I avoid it?
- Do I assume that I can't provide honest and clear advice to someone because I think that individual may not be able to handle it?

The final step in giving feedback is making sure you're understood and that the recipient has all the information needed to improve. We recommend having a system in place that tracks or explicitly states what the expectations are so both parties understand each other. One way to do this is, before ending the conversation, asking for clarification or what the recipient heard or experienced.

The lesson from the fireside chats and these examples for leaders is evident: Connecting and engaging with your employees matters most. To do so you have to show you care and understand. You can encourage and empower people to help improve themselves as well as work together for the common good. Finally, using the best technology available to do so makes it possible.

Today, leaders and HR professionals, working together, have the power to transform both their businesses and the experiences of their employees. The key is tearing down the prior barriers and challenging ourselves to adopt a mindset of abundance—*rather than fear itself*—when it comes to enabling resilient, agile, and engaged employees. And it starts with the tools we use.

One of those tools, which we will describe in detail in the next chapter, is the people development plan, a cornerstone of performance enablement and an incredibly useful tool for an organization seeking to get the most from its people.

Key Takeaways

- Employees want to know that managers and coworkers have their back and can support them in accomplishing their work. Above all, employees want to see how their contributions matter.

- Cultures that switch to giving continuous feedback—in the moment and during regular reviews—will find it difficult if there isn't trust for the system in place. This is why training is so important.

- Sometimes managers or employees will want to check in daily or weekly, and sometimes not. Underpinning the conversations is a procedure by which employees can talk with their managers or peers whenever they need help or support.

- Creating a culture of feedback starts at the top. If the leaders in the company aren't willing to accept feedback, own their mistakes, and be transparent about their own and the company's goals, how then can they expect their employees to do so? Employees need assurance that they are safe to give and receive feedback without fear of retaliation. They need to be able to fail, fail quickly, and be afforded the tools to recover, change, and improve.

CHAPTER 4

Putting Performance Enablement into Practice with People Development Plans

Creating the Perfect People Development Plan

There is no better potential competitive edge than your people, but that can only be realized if you can develop the skills and strengths your people need to move the business forward. To make that happen, you need a comprehensive people development plan.

We believe that creating the perfect employee development plan depends on a consistent, templated process that managers can quickly implement to determine the right direction for employee growth. A people development plan (also known as an employee development or professional development plan) provides direction and focus to help individual employees achieve their long-term professional and career goals. In one easy-to-read document, people development plans gather all the components an employee needs to move their career forward.

People development plans are similar to career development plans but take a much higher-level view and broader scope. Career development plans are tightly focused on the employee's trajectory within their current organization. People development plans set the stage for professional and personal development that employees can also use outside and beyond the organization.

With a people development plan in place, employees can find both their personal strengths and their professional calling. Although people development plans could extend beyond an employee's tenure with your business, cultivating employee growth within your organization encourages employees to remain there, where they're highly valued. We believe the key to building a great organization is not only building a team of teams but also developing the individuals on those teams so that they all feel empowered to act on behalf of the entire organization.

Four Benefits of an Employee Development Plan

Effective people development planning produces positive results for employees and the business. It helps in the following four ways.

Employees Discover New Talents

Following an employee development plan can help team members discover talents and skills they didn't know they had. When creating an employee development plan, team members gain exposure to different areas of the business. For example, part of their development could include picking up projects in different departments, which encourages them to try new things and learn new skills. In addition, opportunities to exercise lesser-used skills can help employees understand what tasks they're best at and most enjoy. When viewed cumulatively, people development plans help you discover workforce strengths that can influence your organizational talent strategy.

As employees and managers track their development plans, the data tells the story of your organization's hidden talents. Your HR team can use this data to assess the workforce's bench strength, inventory the skill sets and abilities being developed by team members, and view where those skills exist within the business. Then, you can use that information to develop succession plans and support other long-term business goals.

Employee Performance Improves Overall

One of the most substantial outcomes of effective people development planning is improved employee performance. As employees develop their skills and work toward their goals, they gain abilities and experiences they can apply to their current work. An enriched skill set enables employees to perform better, producing better outcomes. Additionally, the opportunity to exercise new skills can keep employees interested and engaged in their daily routines. A successful talent strategy depends on optimizing performance so the business can get where it needs to go faster and at a lower cost.

An Organization's Competitive Edge Is Enhanced

People development plans take a broad look at development, both professional and personal. Helping employees develop themselves—as lifelong learners and better communicators, for example—has far-reaching benefits. In addition, people development plans can help existing employees develop the skills, abilities, and knowledge needed to move into new roles in other parts of the business.

Employees committed to a development plan are always growing, which can give businesses a competitive advantage. CEOs and chief human resources officers (CHROs) should commit to developing a workforce that is agile enough to adapt to sudden developments and is resilient in the face of change. The ability to pivot can help you navigate disruptions that might derail other businesses.

Voluntary Turnover Is Reduced

As you know, turnover is one of the costliest expenses for any organization. A robust employee development program creates a culture where employees are curious and constantly acquiring knowledge. Channeling that growth into an employee development plan can provide direction and keep employees engaged in their work. When employees can see where they can grow within the company, they're less likely to leave.

People development plans give the workforce greater visibility into their growth options. In addition, the process of writing out such plans can help employees and managers engage in future-oriented performance conversations and identify development opportunities.

How to Create an Effective Development Plan

The results of people development can only be as effective as your development plan is actionable. Done well and under the leadership of both the CEO and CHRO, HR professionals, managers, and employees can use this collaborative process to revolutionize the workforce. An effective development plan requires that you do the following.

Start with a Skills-Gap Analysis

Before setting a direction for growth, you must determine where growth is most needed. Then, for each employee, conduct a skills-gap analysis to see what areas the worker needs to improve to reach full potential.

In large organizations, it's unlikely that HR can assess each team member individually. This is why team of teams come in handy. Train managers to collaborate with employees to identify skills gaps. Equip managers with talent assessments and other tools that can provide insight into each employee's strengths and opportunities.

Employees should have a voice in the process because they have the best sense of where they struggle the most. And because these discussions can be sensitive and personal, it's helpful if employees are first to raise concerns about their skills gaps. Train managers to have employee-led conversations around this topic.

Identify Growth Opportunities

Gaps indicate opportunities to grow. As employees identify skills gaps, help them determine what they want their employee development plan to target. Prioritize one or two growth opportunities to work toward in the upcoming quarter.

Ask employees about their preferences for growth opportunities. For example, they might want to take a temporary role in another department or to take on added responsibility on their team. Managers can offer direction to help employees determine their focus, by offering input based on observations of the employee's performance.

Develop a Clear Action Plan

One of the most critical pieces of an employee development plan is setting clear tasks to accomplish. Vague goals don't empower employees to act. Instead, employees need to know exactly what steps will take them where they want to go.

Help employees with drafting an action. Action items within this plan might include taking a course, obtaining a certification, or demonstrating mastery of skills in the flow of work through completing a specific task or activity.

Focus on Goal Alignment

The beauty of an employee development plan is that the impact of the plan resonates across the workforce. So as managers and employees explore options for employee growth, ensure that business goals are front and center.

Employees should be able to draw connections between the steps they're taking and the effects on the business. Employees who comprehend broader business goals can understand whether their development fits, draw inspiration from those goals, and align their personal goals with the business's trajectory. Our own research suggests that seeing that connection to the business greatly improves an employee's engagement and productivity. Managers play an essential role in interpreting these business goals and helping employees see what steps they can take to create the most impact.

Consider All Types of Training and Development

Don't limit your idea of what makes an effective training program. Your business houses hundreds of learning opportunities, big and small, formal and informal. Help managers and employees understand the wealth of learning resources available to them.

With this information, managers can more effectively help employees find which resources work best. On-the-job learning, for instance, is a powerful tool for teaching concepts and assisting employees to apply them in real situations. In addition, team members who are kinesthetic learners, who learn by doing, may realize their best results from on-the-job learning.

Establish Ways to Provide Feedback

Ongoing feedback is crucial to the success of any employee development plan. Feedback from managers can help employees gauge whether they're on track or need to reassess their goals.

Managers need tools that enable them to deliver real-time feedback and track those conversations for future reference. Specific communication tools, such as your project enablement platform, can facilitate these conversations. In addition, look for feedback and communication tools that can integrate with existing systems and software.

Creating an Employee Development Plan Template

In addition to training managers to collaborate with employees on their development plans, you can also use a written template to help guide your planning process. These components are essential to include in your employee development plan template.

Long-Term Vision

Each employee's long-term vision for their career is the bedrock of that person's development plan. Employees should clearly understand where they want to go as professionals, even if that vision is subject to change. Managers can help draw out this long-term outlook by asking employees about the work they enjoy most or where they see themselves progressing within the company.

Short-Term Objectives

Employees can also collaborate with managers to develop short-term objectives. These should be goals that the employee can accomplish within a set time frame and that should feed into the long-term vision and support the overall growth of the business and the employee alike.

Goals

Goals are specific outcomes that indicate the employee has met short-term objectives. Goals should be measurable and clearly indicate what the employee has accomplished. If an employee's objective is to gain traction as a thought leader, for example, then landing a public-speaking engagement could be considered a key result related to that objective.

Learning Resources

When creating their development plan, employees should have a list of learning resources to draw on. For example, the list might include suggested courses or documented opportunities to accept gigs in other parts of the organization. Managers should be able to guide employees to the learning opportunities that are most meaningful and useful to them. Keep this list updated regularly, so employees understand their learning options.

People development planning is a crucial piece of an effective talent strategy. To succeed, every manager and employee must have the necessary tools and resources to embrace professional development and, most important, must communicate that information effectively among teams. This requires an action plan.

Employee Action-Plan Examples to Jump-Start Your Engagement Strategy

We liken action plans and employee engagement strategies to your car's ignition. You can meticulously plan a road trip to hit everything you want to see, but until you turn that key and start to drive, all that preparation is nothing but potential energy. Action planning is the key in the ignition; it transforms that potential into reality, turning employee feedback into tangible improvements across your organization.

But action planning isn't necessarily second nature, especially for HR leaders and managers new to employee engagement. Therefore, we're going to build on our employee engagement and development plan and examine some action-plan examples leaders can use as a starting point. Although the action-planning process isn't always instinctual, it isn't necessarily like rocket science. Use these examples and insights to inform your own action plans and start seeing the many benefits of improved engagement.

Creating Your Action Plans

Effective action planning starts by identifying pain points and trends within your organization that you need to address. These could include aspects of your work environment, specific issues with the employee experience or senior leadership, or any number of dynamics in your company. The actual process of identifying these issues depends on your choice of engagement software. To simplify things, however, we'll use Betterworks's platform as an example.

For any given employee survey report in Betterworks, the system tells where you are performing well in your organization and where you need to improve. For instance, if a report reveals that you need to work on Feedback & Recognition, then you can create an action plan directly from the report using a list of prefiltered templates.

Assuming you're using engagement software with integrated action planning, the software will have its own process of identifying areas for improvement. Once you've targeted those areas, it's then time to start creating the actual plans using a series of steps. Choose a leader to supervise and guide the action plan, ensuring the leader is a good fit for the task.

If you are action planning for a larger initiative, divide the overall plan into a series of smaller ones, assigning a leader for each subplan. Because all the smaller plans must work together, be sure to organize everything well according to timelines, tasks, and goals. Once again, the right engagement software can help keep track of these different teams and moving parts and ensure the overall plan stays on track.

Develop clear objectives for every action plan. Use concise language that isn't vague but instead clearly spells out your goals. Establish checkpoints and milestones that HR and the action plan leader can use to monitor progress and direction.

Measuring the Results of Your Action Plan

After you've completed the plan, you need to measure the results and gauge your success. There are a variety of ways to do so, including, but not limited to the following.

Surveys

Surveys are the primary means to measure employee engagement. The initial, longer-form survey and quick follow-up pulse surveys and polls allow you to probe specific issues over time and across the entire organization without human bias.

Using a small number of open-ended questions in your surveys can reveal, through an employee's own words, even deeper insights than strictly sticking to the Likert scale. That response scale is a type of psychometric measurement that entails responders specifying their level of agreement to a statement, typically in five points: (1) strongly disagree, (2) disagree, (3) neither agree nor disagree, (4) agree, and (5) strongly agree (or similar language). Assuming you're using a capable analytics platform with integrated natural language processing (NLP) and machine learning, you can then convert that open-ended feedback into trackable, quantitative data.

Likewise, you can integrate employee Net Promoter Score (eNPS) questions into your survey to consistently gauge the many different factors and drivers needed for engagement. Just like using Net Promoter Score (NPS) with customers, eNPS-based questions will help you measure factors like loyalty and satisfaction over a period to identify trends and areas for improvement.

One-on-Ones

Conducting frequent one-on-one meetings with managers is a more productive and effective form of the traditional annual review. It provides employees with a consistent forum to voice concerns, provide feedback, and, from the manager's perspective, create a valuable touchstone with their team members. Further, as part of a continuous feedback collection strategy, these regular check-ins become crucial in maintaining a healthy, productive, and communicative relationship between a manager and the team members. Naturally, this type of relationship lends itself to greater employee engagement, job satisfaction, productivity, and a variety of other benefits.

Small-Group Discussions and Focus Groups

These discussions provide many of the same benefits as one-on-ones but only from a broader point of view. Managers can run a guided discussion on a specific topic or area of concern that might have stemmed from survey results. It's a way to drill further into issues through an open-forum format.

Technology can help managers maximize results here if they use employee-engagement software like Betterworks to drive these discussions and feedback sessions. These tools give organizations the ability to measure sentiment through feedback conversations and also provide every group member an equally powerful voice.

Interviews Across the Employee Journey

Everyone has heard of exit interviews. They're a mainstay with organizations that want honest feedback on the employee experience from people no longer as concerned about retribution or negative consequences on their careers. However, collecting feedback from every stage of the employee journey is imperative in building a satisfying experience, from the recruitment stage to an employee's last day and beyond.

For instance, onboarding surveys and feedback are instrumental in allowing an organization to better understand the employee experience as a new hire joins the team. The organization can use that feedback to improve the onboarding process continually. Likewise, a relatively new iteration of this concept is the stay interview. Used for the middle stages of the employee journey, stay interviews can help measure things like engagement and satisfaction in a more personal and interactive setting.

Employee Recognition

Recognition is a more indirect but still important barometer for overall engagement levels. Whether you use a designated employee-recognition platform or a more organic strategy, the frequency of recognition and both the recognized and recognizers can indicate where you fall in engagement levels. As a general rule, the more recognition taking place, the more your people are engaged. Although this is one of the more imprecise ways to measure engagement among the different methods we've discussed thus far, recognition can still provide a thumbnail sketch of your overall engagement levels.

Metrics

Organizations already track a set of metrics to monitor their operations, revenue, profitability, and other key measures. However, metrics go far beyond sales margins and break-even points. A few specific metrics can give employers at least a loose idea of engagement levels within the enterprise. Granted, they cannot afford the in-depth, comprehensive insights that specialized tools provide. Still, certain metrics are useful, including those measuring engagement return on investment (ROI), diversity and inclusion, eNPS, absenteeism, employee turnover, satisfaction, and alignment indicators between employee goals and the company mission.

For the most revealing and valuable results, companies should pair these metrics with surveys, one-on-ones, and some other ways to measure engagement. Together, these form a comprehensive engagement strategy that lets HR measure and track engagement from multiple angles and perspectives.

Measuring Employee Engagement: Best Practices and Common Mistakes

To help you get the most from your engagement strategy, we have some dos and don'ts to keep in mind when measuring engagement levels within your organization.

Dos

- Start your engagement strategy with a plan and goals before distributing your initial survey. Then let the survey results inform and guide your path in the future.
- Follow up your initial survey with consistent pulse surveys of three to five questions as well as one-question polls. This approach will help you identify progress as you continue to measure your results.
- Use follow-up pulse surveys and polls to drill down into issues within specific employee segments and stages of the employee experience.

Don'ts

- Bombard your employees with endless surveys. After your initial survey, keep it short and to the point. Survey fatigue is real and can quickly impede any efforts to measure and improve employee engagement.
- Narrow your focus on specific employee segments with your longer-form surveys. Use your follow-ups for drilling down, not your more extensive and comprehensive surveys.
- Forget to use open-ended questions. Granted, this might not be feasible for larger organizations that don't use a capable engagement and analytics platform. However, the combination of the Likert scale and open-ended questions will give you the most in-depth, representative picture of engagement levels across your company.
- Rely exclusively on surveys. Although they form the foundation of any effective engagement strategy, they're best when accompanied by one-on-ones with managers, small discussion

groups, employee-recognition programs, and the other measurement tools we discussed.

Employee-Centric Experiences in the Flow of Work

It's critical that any application you want or expect employees to use on a regular basis be easily accessible, intuitive to navigate, and, ideally, integrated into the flow of how an employee gets work done each day. Most desk employees will find most their time spent in email and messaging applications, where communication with colleagues, managers, and customers takes place most frequently. When your software for goals, conversations, feedback, and recognition is kept totally separate, locked away in a human resources information system (HRIS), and only accessed once a year, not only are these practices *not* top of mind, but also you are, in essence, asking employees to develop their own systems for keeping track of their work, development plans, feedback they'd like to give or request, and people they'd like to thank and recognize. Of course, most people in the course of their regular busy workday aren't going to do that. So, performance processes are neglected, and annual conversations continue to be ineffective vehicles for assessing an entire year's worth of contribution.

Software for performance enablement does things differently. Goals you can see and update from your Gmail inbox, however, become actionable reminders of where to focus your energy and time. Conversation templates you can view and edit from your Outlook calendar become thoughtful agendas that form the basis for meaningful conversations. Recognition that the entire company can see in your company Slack channel can reinforce your cultural values and engage employees.

As a leader, when you're able to view progress in real time and in the flow of work, you can ultimately empower team members throughout the organization to make faster, better decisions that lead to business impact. Offering feedback in the flow of work helps you address behaviors in real time. Employees will make a better connection between what you're telling them and how they can improve moving forward. The feedback that occurs in real time comes across as more genuine and prevents surprises for employees when formal evaluations do occur.

Key Takeaways

- The people development plan is an excellent tool for getting the most out of employees, in large part because it takes seriously their goals for their own individual careers in addition to how they can contribute to the company at large.
- Your people give you the best competitive edge, in our view, but only if you can develop the skills, abilities, and strengths your people need to move the business forward. To make that happen, you need a comprehensive people development plan.
- The results of people development can only be as effective as your development plan is actionable. Done well, under the leadership of both the CEO and CHRO, HR professionals, managers, and employees can use this collaborative process to revolutionize the workforce.
- A plan that suits your organization can open the eyes of everyone, from the newest hire to the executive, to how they can secure more effective training, how the company can reenvision its goals, and essentially how the individual and the institution can serve one another more effectively.

- The key to effective use of a people development plan is communication. Maximize effective interactions between managers and employees, and ensure that executives are accessible to all.

CHAPTER 5

Leading Your Performance Transformation

After You've Measured Engagement

Measuring employee engagement is ongoing and builds on itself. One iteration of surveys, polls, and subsequent action plans leads into the next, meaning that if you're diligent, you're continually identifying areas for improvement and boosting engagement levels.

Just remember, putting a sound strategy in place doesn't do much good if you're not following up with a targeted action plan. Measure the results of your ongoing stream of feedback, analyze and act on them, and then repeat the process. This is the best way to make employee engagement a fundamental part of your organization, just as relevant and impactful as financial reporting, research and development (R&D), or any of the other critical components of your operations.

Building Momentum with Quick Wins

After you distribute your initial employee engagement survey, collect the results, and analyze the survey data, there's a fair chance you'll end up with several different areas for improvement. While that's to be expected, particularly for companies just starting their engagement strategy, it leaves you with a decision to make: Where should you start with your action planning?

We usually suggest targeting the low-hanging fruit first, the quick wins that will help you build momentum. Once you have some success under your belt and employees see that you're committed to making improvements, that momentum can sustain you as you tackle more complex issues down the road.

For example, let's say your employee survey results show that you should focus on the management engagement driver—a gauge on an employee's experience and relationship with their direct supervisor—in your accounting department. Perhaps people in accounting feel that their team leader is too distant, making it an area for improvement. HR can take these action items from your survey report, sit down with that team leader and maybe even the leader's supervisor, and devise a simple but effective action plan to start addressing the issue.

Obviously, this example is very straightforward and doesn't require much preparation. However, the simple act of personal interaction can make an employee feel appreciated and valued by the manager, even if it only lasts a few moments. According to research, supervisors account for 70 percent of variance in individual engagement levels.[1] In other words, even these quick wins can have a significant impact on employee engagement in your organization.

Extending that example, let's assume your survey report also revealed a lack of clarity from that same accounting manager regarding messages from company leaders. Once again, an action plan built around the management or communication engagement drivers can address this issue.

If employees feel like they're getting muddled information or unclear direction from the direct supervisor on company-wide initiatives or even departmental goals, *skip-level meetings* (between team members and their supervisors' boss) can help clarify that message. Research indicates that roughly 50 percent of employees are not entirely clear on their responsibilities at work, so this type of action plan is increasingly common in companies.

Action Planning for Bigger Initiatives

Of course, some action plans are inherently more complex than others, especially when dealing with more significant engagement initiatives. Therefore, we're going to continue our previous example, assuming that the lack of clarity in leadership messaging wasn't just identified in accounting and several workgroups.

These results indicate more of a systemic issue—that is, people throughout the company feel a lack of communication from senior leaders. Scheduling skip-level meetings in every department is a good first step, but if the underlying problem is more extensive than just an issue with managers, then you will want to adopt an action plan that's bigger in scope and reach.

This is a perfect example of a larger plan you could supplement or divide into smaller plans. For example, someone would have to organize the actual town hall meetings, and managers would need to plan short follow-ups with their teams. Each of these might require its own action plan. And naturally, the bigger the organization, the more complex the planning would be.

Whatever you're targeting with your employee-engagement action plans, ensure they address the areas of concern from your survey results. Start small and build on your successes, expanding the scope of your action planning as you become more comfortable with the process. With time, you'll see improvements in employee engagement levels that can propel the entire organization forward.

Vertiv Improves Employee Engagement and Shifts the Culture

Vertiv is an American provider of equipment and services for data centers. In 2016, Platinum Equity acquired the Emerson Network Power business from Emerson Electric and rebranded it as Vertiv. Headquartered in Columbus, Ohio, Vertiv employs twenty-four thousand people in over 130 countries, where it has manufacturing and assembly facilities. It also has regional headquarters in England, Italy, the Philippines, China, and India. The company became publicly traded on the New York Stock Exchange (NYSE) through a merger with GS Acquisition Holdings in 2020. Going through a period of transition, they decided to completely transform their people processes to drive engagement, build a culture of transparency, and create individual goals that aligned with the organization.

When Vertiv was spun off from Emerson, it faced significant challenges aligning employee goals to company strategy and lacked a shared vision and culture. As a result, employee morale dipped dangerously low. With an eNPS of -23 percent, the company had no effective performance-management processes in place. Vertiv brought on Betterworks shortly after it was spun out of Emerson Electric. At the time, Vertiv had no consistent HR processes globally, transparency was low, and a culture of mistrust prevailed. It was also transforming its business from product-oriented to solution-oriented and recognized a need to develop its people to meet the changing business needs.

In order to turn the proverbial ship around, Kate Beatty, Vertiv's global vice president, Learning and Development, focused mainly on the "conversation" and building engagement the first year Vertiv rolled out its employee-engagement plan. "We focused less so on OKRs and goals and more on whether or not managers and employees were having frequent conversations and trying to help managers have those conversations." The reason for doing so, she explained, was that Vertiv had a history as an organization that had been defined by uncertainty and change. The employees, she said, began to believe that they'd "just wait, and this will all pass." She wanted to ensure the employees could see that the culture was shifting again but this time transformationally to the Vertiv of today.

This public company is serious about employee success and engagement. Beatty recognized Vertiv employees needed much more connection, which the company provided by emphasizing quarterly feedback conversations, regular team meetings, and one-on-ones.

On the Betterworks application, Vertiv listed what it wanted managers and employees to focus on. Employee resilience was one such area. How were employees able to manage their work life and the boundary between home and work? This conversation allowed managers to see people and help them work through challenges. Vertiv focused specifically on building the relationship between the managers and employees to better ensure managers were coaching their employees effectively. After five years of practicing that renewed emphasis on relationships and coaching, over 90 percent of their employees completed their quarterly conversations, with nearly 85 percent of their respondents saying the conversations were beneficial.

In their employee engagement surveys, managers received high marks as effective leaders. In 2020, managers played a crucial role in easing the transition to remote work and communicating with employees through a challenging environment. In January 2021 it filled three positions on the executive team with internal promotions, including a CHRO.

CEOs Who Get It

Vertiv's CEO is someone who gets it—that is, Vertiv instilled a CHRO at the C-suite level and, as in the case of Adobe, the CHRO reports to the CEO and is empowered to build and support its HR team in a way that supports managers to develop employees. This in turn drives the company culture to one that focuses on transparent, honest, and frequent conversations. With these conversations and feedback, CEO and CHRO understand what skills are required in order to thrive, build future leaders, and improve the company's overall performance.

You will drive bottom-line impact and build a strong culture if you are brave enough to make such changes. The last thing a CEO wants is to know their organization is no longer competitive, that it doesn't have the right skills or people. Your company is no longer performing at the level it did. The only way to remain competitive is to have a CHRO beside you who can help you empower your company's most important resource—people. You need to have the right partner by your side to get you there; otherwise, you'll find yourself alongside companies like Borders and Blockbuster. The right HR leader in an organization can give you the competitive edge you need and can be a game-changer.

Unfortunately, as we've seen a lot, HR leaders are devalued. We want to challenge CEOs, board members, and other leaders to rethink and reimagine HR's role. We also recommend rotating other leaders in your organization into HR.

We believe great leaders can be found in any role. They can figure out what's required where they are and gain a better understanding of the role by having been in the position. And yes, sometimes this causes disruption, but sometimes disruption is precisely what is needed to facilitate change.

Asking the Right Questions

Successful organizations need a committed worker in HR to partner with the CEO to execute their goals. That means HR needs to have a seat at the table. CEOs and CHROs working together, just as Indra and Cynthia did (discussed subsequently), will harness the potential of all employees. One way to see if your company or organization is aligned strategically is to see who the CHRO reports to. If he or she reports to the CFO, then you need to reconsider your organization because that usually indicates that the CEO put the HR leader there to avoid dealing with those "human resources issues" (read: tactical issues). The CHROs who have complete discretion over their budgets have the freedom to choose and adapt in the moment to shift priorities. A CEO should consider the CHRO as a partner, often the closest one.

We think every executive considering being a CHRO should ask the following questions before accepting the new position:

- Whom will I be reporting to?
- What is my operating budget?
- Am I on the executive team? And will I be in all executive meetings where key decisions are made?
- What are the strategic roles that I will be playing to help the company achieve its goals?

In our minds, the best CHRO will work right beside the CEO and everyone on the board and will constantly ask questions and understand what the company is trying to accomplish. That CHRO will challenge the CEO as a leader and will call even the best of the company out for playing favorites. A great CHRO will hold a mirror up to a CEO, remind him or her what the goals are, and challenge that person: "Does your leadership team have the skills that will get you there?"

Conversely, the worst type of person running HR and performance management in the company is one who only hangs out with HR friends. That person doesn't have an interest in the business or the overall strategies. Instead, the HR leader thinks he or she is helping the company by being "compliant"—that is, filling seats, keeping the employees happy, and preventing the company from being sued. This individual thinks in black and white and makes all decisions within the lines of the policies. The executive slows the organization down, making managers create loads of documentation to support a termination. Overall, this HR professional lacks business acumen and may not even define him- or herself as being a part of the organization's business.

When Doug was at Cisco, he worked with many different HR business partners. Over the course of his eleven years there, he knew when he had an HR business partner who would add value to him and help him achieve his goals. He also knew which ones made his life difficult, especially when it came time for him to let go of poor performers. It also became apparent to Doug that when a leader empowers HR by giving a seat at the table, then HR is able to hold up a mirror to the leader. The HR leader is unafraid to share knowledge of what's happening in the organization. A great CHRO will know the causes behind the issues the CEO doesn't know about.

Of course, HR leaders at Cisco should care, be curious, and want to understand employees. Cisco's vision statement was "We change the way people will live, work, learn, and play." Doug was so proud of what his former employer did. The company literally built the internet. Cisco made it possible for X-rays to be sent directly into operating rooms. It is the core of Wall Street and of the trading floor for the largest stock exchanges around the world. Cisco did change the way everyone lived. If Cisco had an HR person fundamentally uninterested in that or in the vision of the company, that individual would have been wrong for the role.

CHROs need to see the big picture and their part in it. When a CHRO is interested in and passionate about the company and operates from a place where the company's vision is always front and center, that creates a completely different strategy. That HR person is operationally focused to help the *entire* organization thrive. That CHRO would ask these questions:

- Are we looking far enough into the future and looking at what new skills will be required in the shifting landscape?
- Do we have the right people, skill sets, attitudes, and culture to take us there?
- Are we agile enough to still fulfill our purpose if things don't go as planned (because of disruptors like a global pandemic, increased working from home, the Great Resignation, recessions, inflations, natural disasters)?
- What are we doing today to attract the right people for tomorrow's jobs?
- Do we have the proper tools, systems, and processes to support these initiatives?

What the Best Leaders Do

The best thing a leader can do is embody the changes he wants to see in his teams. Over Doug's long and storied career as a leader, he has created a running list of values he thinks a strong leader needs to embody to drive change, influence others effectively, and build a strong team (what he believes is a leader's number one job). A strong leader does the following:

- Leads with empathy and truly cares about people.
- Holds very high standards for him- or herself and the people around them.
- Delivers on commitments.
- Acts with integrity at all times.
- Has self-confidence, not arrogance.
- Is sincere.
- Makes decisions in the best interest of the company every time.
- Thinks cross-functionally, not just about their own function; thinks like the CEO.
- Makes fiduciary decisions for the company and, as such, understands the magnitude of that and what is and isn't affordable.
- Possesses the people skills to help individuals or the team understand the reason for decisions, even though they may still disagree.
- Makes hard decisions with the right amount of input and doesn't always seek consensus.
- Balances internal and external hires.
- Is always looking for new talent to bring into the company.
- Understands the value of, and builds, diverse teams and thinks globally.
- Knows how long to work with an individual on issues before moving on.
- Understands that change is sometimes needed.

- Is a student of business, technology, and people.
- Seeks the advice of many.
- Asks for help and second opinions.
- Is a life learner.
- Communicates proactively with other executives to understand and involve them in the thought process, not just to convey the outcome.
- Manages their manager.
- Offers insights into the business, including what is going well and what is not.
- Is not looking to be well liked but rather to be well respected.
- Has the confidence to evaluate his management team and understands and can articulate the good and bad, along with plans to address them.
- Does not undermine the team's decision, once the CEO offers an opinion. Gets in the boat and supports the decision 100 percent. If the choice fails, refrains from saying, "I told you so."
- Praises publicly and criticizes privately.
- Gives opinions, without waiting to be asked.
- Asks people how they are doing if he or she doesn't know.

Ultimately, the greatest leaders enable others to disrupt and facilitate growth, innovation, and change. When CEOs empower others to make decisions for themselves on behalf of the company because they know what the company's goals are, what the CEO's goals are, and what the vision for the company is, those leaders begin to think of themselves as strategic partners for the CEO.

We bet if we asked ten CEOs who their most valued strategic partner is, they might mention their COO, CFO, general counsel, or CIO. It might take a few titles to get to CHRO. A great CHRO is your team of rivals and team of teams all in one. That CHRO will tell you what you need to hear, not what you want to hear. That CHRO has boots on the ground and knows what is going on with the people and the culture in a way no one else does.

We challenge you today. How is your HR functioning in your organization? Are you thinking about it correctly? Is it a game-changing function? And if not, why not? What are you doing about it?

If HR isn't reporting to the CEO, it should. If you think you've got the wrong leader in the position, don't be afraid to change. Now is the time.

From a Team of Rivals to a Team of Teams

During one of the most contentious times in American history, Abraham Lincoln was elected to lead a country on the brink of civil war. Knowing he couldn't lead the country out of crisis alone, he assembled a cabinet that could meet the demands of the day. To the surprise of everyone, especially his friends and fellow party members, Lincoln made seats at the table for several individuals who differed from him politically in every conceivable way. But Lincoln wasn't simply looking for yes men. Instead, he wanted to assemble a team of the strongest leaders with a wide range of opinions. He realized that having strong leaders with their own expertise and different views than his own would not only sharpen his thinking but also help him make headway in ultimately uniting the country.

What he did when he assembled this cabinet of advisers was unprecedented. No president before him filled the cabinet with opposing party members (and few have done so since—at least in such a dramatic fashion). Prior to Lincoln, the idea had always been that a president needed to be surrounded by people who thought like him—and the ruling party. Lincoln disagreed. He knew with so much change happening and so much division in the country, he needed to understand where both sides were coming from, and he needed to be able to connect with them.

Doris Kearns Goodwin, author of the Pulitzer Prize–winning and bestselling book *Team of Rivals: The Political Genius of Abraham Lincoln*, argues that a set of emotional strengths was the foundation of Lincoln's leadership abilities. According to Goodwin, Lincoln understood that human relations were vital to the success of a leader. If Lincoln wanted to lead his country through a civil war, he had to be able to lead a smaller team effectively first. He knew this would require sensitivity, empathy, compassion, kindness, and radical honesty— from both him and his team. Lincoln made time for each of his cabinet members, so that they all felt they had access to him. He treated them all respectfully and fairly and even formed unlikely friendships with his staunchest critics. Ultimately, he gained all their respect in turn. He exemplified in his own life what he wanted the people he was leading to do—to come together for the sake of the whole.

About 155 years after Lincoln took office and assembled his team of rivals, General Stanley McChrystal wrote a book on the power of coming together for the sake of something greater: *Team of Teams: New Rules of Engagement for a Complex World*. In the early 2000s, Gen. McChrystal commanded the Joint Special Operations Command for the US forces and began to see that the world that leaders were operating in was changing; therefore, leadership styles needed to adapt and change. Building from Lincoln's notion that the president should have access to the greatest minds and expertise by essentially assembling a team, McChrystal further argued that the key to success for any leader was the ability to not only build their own team but empower those teams to build teams in a similar fashion. He maintained that teams needed to be extremely transparent when sharing information and decentralized with decision-making authority, meaning that team members would be empowered to act without express written authority and could command a situation as needed. Gen. McChrystal also advocated building a team of teams because it would be better suited to respond to a hyperconnected and rapidly changing world. He believed that the structure of a team of teams would be more like a coral reef than a pyramid—that is, like a coral reef, organizations could reconfigure and adapt on a moment's notice rather than wait for the order to trickle down from on high, like it might in a pyramid-shaped hierarchical organization. This structure creates more agile and, therefore, less fragile organizations. But it requires leaders and CEOs to do as he and Lincoln did: trust others to get the important jobs done and give them a seat at the table to do so.

HR Empowered to Make Decisions

In 2016 David Burkus of *Forbes* interviewed Donna Morris, then senior vice president of HR at Adobe, to discuss the impact of her decision to ditch performance reviews at the company. Morris revealed, surprisingly, that *she didn't ask* the CEO's permission. And it wasn't a case of "ask for forgiveness later, not permission now" that we often hear about in the business world. In this case, there was nothing to forgive. Morris didn't need to ask permission, even if she surprised herself when she made the pronouncement.

After all, her decision did seem off-the-cuff. According to Morris, she had traveled to India to meet with colleagues and spend time at Adobe's offices. Jet-lagged, sleep-deprived, and frazzled, she hadn't been in the country long when she agreed to be interviewed by a reporter from India's *Economic Times*. When the reporter asked Morris what she could do to disrupt HR, Morris responded immediately, "We plan to abolish the annual performance review format."[2]

The paper ran with her quote the next day and the headline Adobe Systems Set to Scrap Annual Appraisals, to Rely on Regular Feedback to Reward Staff. The only problem was Morris hadn't yet sat down with Adobe's CEO, Shantanu Narayen, to discuss this change with him.[3]

However, her remark wasn't actually entirely off-the-cuff. Morris had been thinking about the issue for some time. And it wasn't as if she was speaking out of turn or without Narayen's approval. When Narayen hired her, he had bestowed that approval. He trusted her to run her team the way she needed to on behalf of the whole organization.

In another interview with Adam Bryant, senior manager for the ExCo Group, Morris said, "I personally would not have taken the job unless the HR function reports to the CEO. It's a nonstarter otherwise. If HR reports to the CFO, you're going to get a cost-based HR leader who is removed from making objective decisions."[4]

She didn't stop there. Morris went on to say, "The head of HR should not only report to the CEO but should also have a core relationship with the board of directors. The HR function should be pretty independent, just like Audit is on the board. If you really are going to act as an ombudsman for the effective operation of your organization, you have to feel like you can push back against your peers and even the CEO."[5]

From day one at Adobe, she made it clear that she had what she called "a seat at the table." She didn't have to wait for the CEO's permission to shake up HR at Adobe. Instead, she had been empowered from day one to do so. And, as she said, "I'm not going to sit around and not have a voice. It's just not who I am."[6]

Like many HR leaders, Morris took her role seriously and knew just how valuable a CHRO could be to improving the company's overall performance. She did her due diligence before taking the job. She asked many of the questions we also recommended earlier in chapter 4 and ended up working with a CEO and leadership team for which she could make such bold decisions without blowback.

Doug has been selling HR software for many years to all kinds of companies and has seen firsthand when an effective leader in HR has the support of the CEO, versus an HR leader who doesn't or an HR leader who holds a mirror up to the CEO and makes suggestions on the strategy to get the person to be an effective leader. He's also seen the impact these different types of leaders have on the company's performance.

But we know many CHROs aren't in the same position. Many CEOs underestimate how a strong HR leader can impact the company overall. In the article aptly titled "HR: From Paper Pushers to Game Changers," Grant Freeland, a contributor to *Forbes*, writes, "Human resources, once the forgotten stepchild of corporate culture, is poised to become the game changer."[7] He's not wrong. He argues that, just as many who worked in "personnel" couldn't transition to HR in the 1980s, the challenge for HR leaders now is to transition to the new world of technology and people management and understand where those worlds collide. He adds, "Business leaders have a huge stake in this sea change. If they don't embrace it or are not part of it, their business is in trouble. Worse, they may not even realize it: But in this new world, the best HR talent will attract the best talent in other disciplines. And with talent at a premium, who can afford to miss out?"[8]

The answer is no one. But many are still slow to change. We think the main reason is that many CEOs have worked in organizations where HR played a tactical role. They have never seen what it's like to work with a strategic HR leader and what a game-changer it can be. When you find an HR person, who, like Morris, is a mobilizer—that is, someone who is intellectually curious about the business, who thinks like a CEO, and who envisions where the company needs to be five years from now—you have discovered an unstoppable force. This force can take your company beyond anywhere you previously imagined. We know, without a doubt, that the best-performing companies are the ones that make a seat at the table for HR.

Maximizing Your Return on Investment in Strategic CHROs

In her interview with Bryant, Morris says, "The success of a company, for the most part, is always going to come down to the investment you make in people in leadership. I don't know how it doesn't."[9] Like Morris, we know a company's success (and failure) comes down to one thing: people. You can have the best product in the world, but if you don't know how to lead and inspire people to perform, you're not going to survive. No one needs to look very far these days for examples of poor leaders who lack any understanding of how important their people are to their overall success. Elon Musk only needed a couple of weeks as CEO in late 2022 to decimate morale, tank the stock, and lose users on Twitter.

Morris also contends that the majority of CEOs spend a "dispro-portionate amount of time" fixated on financials or the core product and business rather than what their organization really looks like.[10] She wonders if CEOs are looking critically at their company and asking, "Is it designed for success? Do they have the right players? Are they invest-ing enough in developing the leaders of the future? Do they invest as much time in people and leadership as they do in other areas?"

We argue the majority don't. For example, 65 percent of CEOs and organizations still use outdated annual performance review pro-cesses. Therefore, it's safe to say the majority aren't looking closely and critically at how their organization is operating and developing people.

Morris says it best: "If you want to lead a successful company, your core asset is the people who work for you. What have you done for them lately? Have you heard from them? Have you spent enough time thinking about how the company is structured and what kind of tal-ent you're attracting?"[11]

This also goes for the board of directors. Board members, not just CEOs, need to meet with the CHRO. This is the time for all to get on the same page—do the members understand the organizational health of the company? Is the board aware of the performance of the CEO and their reports? Are board members up to speed with the onboarding of any key leaders or succession planning? And if board members don't know these answers, the directors aren't paying close enough attention to the CHRO or valuing and respecting that lead-er's role in the organization.

Morris clearly knows what she is doing. Before her overhaul, Adobe wasted an estimated eighty thousand hours of its managers' time each year to conduct the annual performance reviews, equivalent to about forty full-time employees working all year round.[12]

Not only did switching save the company money, but it also increased employee retention. Before Morris's overhaul, Adobe saw a spike in voluntary attrition every year following annual reviews. Morris attributed those losses to "disappointed employees deciding to leave after receiving ratings below their expectations."[13]

But one of the best and seemingly unexpected outcomes was how employees began to feel about feedback. By switching to lightweight check-ins, morale increased, and it even changed how employees felt about their jobs. Instead of dreading or loathing annual performance reviews, the employees now saw "feedback as a gift." As a result, Adobe eventually saw a 30 percent decrease in the number of employees quitting. It also let go of low performers much more efficiently instead of having to wait for the following annual review. As Gen. McChrystal put it, companies that have the competitive edge are going to remain more agile, and Adobe did just that.

One of the best ways to stay agile is to build teams that can adapt, grow, and develop, and that, too, requires a strategy.

Key Takeaways

- We know, without a doubt, the best-performing companies are the ones that make a seat at the table for HR.
- A strategically focused HR leader shares the long-term vision of the CEO and the company. The best CHRO is going to be a true partner of the CEO and will work right beside him or her, and everyone on the board. That CHRO will constantly ask questions and understand what the company is trying to accomplish.
- Strategic HR leaders match the overall business strategy and goals and align their objectives to those goals—talent

recruitment, retention, company culture, and, of course, work benefits and compliance.

- Strategic HR leaders try to anticipate any challenges and needs but simultaneously plan for adaptability if the business demands it.

- A strategic HR leader is always prepared to ask, "How is this supporting the business? Why would the business care if we do this?"

- A great CHRO is going to challenge the CEO as a leader. That individual will call out even the best of the company for playing favorites. A great CHRO will hold a mirror up to a CEO, remind that leader what the company goals are, and ask, "Does your leadership team have the skills that will get you there?"

- Putting a sound strategy in place doesn't do much good if you're not following up with a targeted action plan. Measure the results of your ongoing stream of feedback, analyze and act on them, and then repeat the process. This is the best way to make employee engagement a fundamental part of your organization, just as relevant and impactful as financial reporting, R&D, or any of the other critical components of your operations.

- The greatest leaders enable others to disrupt the status quo and facilitate growth, innovation, and change. When CEOs empower others to make decisions by themselves on behalf of the company—because they know the company's goals, the CEO's goals, and the CEO's vision for the company—they begin to think of themselves as a strategic partner for the CEO.

- HR leaders want support, strategic alignment with their leaders, and useful data to support their leaders' desire to know what's happening in a company. They also want to be more efficient so that the company can focus on high-value strategic initiatives rather than administrative tasks and processes.
- The most important quality in a CEO today is empathy. If businesses are going to evolve, especially in this postpandemic, economically unstable, and rapidly changing technological world, they will need to respond better to the call for a human-centered and empathic approach.
- Leaders and HR would serve each other and their companies best if they partnered together to strategically align and reimagine how work is done to meet this need.
- Executives need to know what their employees' and teams' goals are, what they're doing, where they're going, and what their needs are.

CHAPTER 6

Implementing Performance Enablement

Chop Wood, Carry Water

In the 1990s there was no better-known or celebrated basketball player than Michael Jordan. He wasn't just considered the best player for the Chicago Bulls; he was thought by many to be the best player in the NBA. Even as a rookie in 1984–1985, Jordan averaged 28.2 points a game. He played all eighty-two games and scored more points than *any* player in the NBA that year—even more than Celtics great Larry Bird and Lakers legend Magic Johnson. Yet, despite Jordan's impressive record, the Bulls didn't bring home the championship that year. Having a player pictured on the Wheaties box, that player's name appearing on a line of sneakers, and having his silhouetted image dunking a basketball on a T-shirt worn by many children in America didn't guarantee future wins either. After all, more than one player carries a team to victory.

Enter Phil Jackson, the newly hired head coach of the Chicago Bulls, who was brought in by the team's owners to figure out how to get more *W*s out of this dazzling basketball star. Jackson did his homework. He watched the Bulls play together and saw that the strategy of the previous coach, Doug Collins, was myopic and centered the Bulls' offense around Michael Jordan. Collins was essentially focusing on the individual wins (mainly for Jordan) and not the big picture. He let Jordan take the shots and urged the team to defer to him on the court.

It doesn't take a wizard to figure out how a defense might prepare for a player like Jordan. Every time Jordan stepped on the court, the defense pounded him. Jackson knew this strategy would never allow the team to win a conference championship. So, he flipped the former coach's strategy on its head. Rather than running an offense that focused only on the best player, Jackson wanted to create one that brought the best out of *each* player on the court. He instituted the triangle offense, a strategy in which every player counts and everyone has the freedom to be the best within a well-specified structure.

Jordan bristled at this at first. He was arguably the best player the game of basketball had ever seen. Why, then, was he being punished? Why was he being told to hold back and let others shine? Jackson asked Jordan, more or less, "Do you want a lifetime of MVPs, but no championship, or do you want to win a championship ring?" Jordan was no loser. Of course he wanted that ring. As a skilled coach, Jackson guided Jordan away from being the best player to being an integral player on the best team.

Interestingly, to do this, Jackson's strategy required that he get to know all players well—what were their motivations, weaknesses, and strengths? He tuned into what each player needed and customized his coaching practices for each. He knew his wild child, Dennis Rodman, would burst if he didn't get to release steam. He sanctioned last-minute trips to Vegas before games, because he knew Rodman would perform better if he was able to get away for a night. Jackson also fine-tuned the Bulls' practice strategy and focused on the fundamentals—tactics. He made what he called the "mundane" into "sacred" rituals. He started running drills as a team, meditating as a team, and even dressing and eating together as a team. He spoke about these fundamentals and tactics. In his book *Eleven Rings: The Soul of Success*, Jackson writes, "There's a Zen saying I often cite that goes, 'Before enlightenment, chop wood, carry water. After enlightenment, chop wood, carry water.' The point: Stay focused on the task at hand rather than dwelling on the past or worrying about the future." There was nothing else to do but "chop wood, carry water"—conditioning, running the drills, practicing the shots, making each good ball player into the best player. When the best players were a team with an aligned strategy or goal (in the Bulls' case, to be the best team and win a championship), anything was possible.

Organizations and businesses all over the world are similarly missing the forest for the trees. They are overly focused on recruiting and retaining high performers (like Jordan) and yanking perceived low performers (like Rodman)—to the point that they're missing out on the opportunity to cultivate a strategy that can bring out the best in every "player" on their teams. Imagine if Jackson coached as his predecessor did, focusing only on his top performer? And imagine if Jackson had seen Dennis Rodman's behavior as so aberrant and toxic to the team that he yanked him. Imagine if Jackson hadn't focused on the other team members on the court—Scottie Pippin, Steve Kerr, and Horace Grant—like so many organizations don't in the name of winning or seeking high performance.

One of the key ways organizations are remiss is in recognizing the need for leaders, specifically heads of HR, who, like Jackson, can embrace both strategic and tactical approaches to performance management or enablement. As Sun Tzu, the Chinese military strategist and philosopher, wrote some twenty-five hundred years ago, "Strategy without tactics is the slowest route to victory. Tactics without strategy is the noise before the defeat." If Jackson had focused solely on the strategy and abandoned the individual needs and gifts of each player, the Bulls would not have won a championship. And if he only focused on the fundamentals, without a bigger strategy or singular goal for the entire team, Jordan may have been an MVP, but he'd never have earned any championship rings.

Strategy versus Tactics: The Benefits of an Operational HR Team

Most, if not all, HR leaders and CEOs believe they are strategic, or thinking in terms of the company's operation. After all, strategy simply means having long-term goals and a plan to achieve them. However, as a CEO (Doug) and HR leader (Jamie), we can vouch that many organizations don't have a strategy. They have a set of tactics, or concrete, small steps, or what businesses love to call "initiatives." They believe they're being strategic, but often they're playing a short game, rather than a long one. In other words, they're looking for Jordans to carry the team, rather than looking for a team to carry each other and the organization. Phil Jackson married both—he thought strategically and acted tactically. So should every organization when hiring a chief human resources officer.

Most companies and their leaders don't differentiate between tactical HR and strategic HR. The main component of a strategic HR leader is to share the long-term vision of the CEO and the company. The leader considers, first, the overall business strategy and goals and then aligns their objectives to those goals—talent recruitment, retention, company culture, and, of course, work benefits and compliance. The HR leader addresses these issues through the lens of years—not weeks or even months. This person tries to anticipate any challenges and needs, but simultaneously plan for adaptability if the business demands it. He or she also relies on data and analytics, rather than personal preferences or biases, and asks tough questions, which keep the objectives aligned with the overall organization's strategy. When Jamie worked at Canadian Tire, she had the privilege of meeting one of the best HR practitioners she's ever met. She recalls during the middle of an HR meeting, this executive interrupted and asked, "How is this supporting the business? Why would the business care if we do this?" This became a mantra for Jamie too in her own career in HR.

Conversely, tactical HR leaders focus primarily on the immediate needs of the organization and department. They put out fires. They hire and onboard new employees as the need arises, handle grievances and harassment complaints, and focus on updating job descriptions, executing surveys, and training employees. Most of their day is spent administrating and keeping the company compliant, by creating and enforcing company policies.

Both strategic and tactical approaches require an incredible amount of time and resources. We've found in our research that the companies that perform best employ both. They have both vision (big-picture strategy) and the ability to execute (tactical strategies). One of the best leaders we know of today who exemplifies leading an organization with both strategic and tactical approaches is the former CEO of PepsiCo, Indra Nooyi.

PepsiCo's Transformational Approach to Performance with a Purpose

Indra K. Nooyi became the first woman of color to lead a Fortune 50 Company, PepsiCo, where she served until 2019. Her strategic thinking, insight into consumer behavior, and wisdom on managing a vast, global workforce make her one of the world's most sought-after advisers to entrepreneurs, executives, and governments. The author of the *New York Times* bestselling *My Life in Full: Work, Family, and Our Future*, Nooyi is an esteemed role model and leader who believes "greatness comes not from a position, but from helping build the future." She is a firm believer that leaders have what she calls an "obligation to pull others up."

While at PepsiCo, she was the chief architect of Performance with Purpose, the company's mission to deliver sustained growth by making more nutritious products, limiting the company's environmental footprint, and empowering its associates and people in the communities it serves. She has been awarded the Padma Bhushan, India's third-highest civilian honor; the US State Department's award for Outstanding American by Choice; and fifteen honorary degrees. Indra is consistently ranked among the world's most powerful women by *Forbes*.

Although overseeing billion-dollar acquisitions and growing PepsiCo, Indra was most recognized for her strategic redirection Performance with a Purpose. She wanted every employee to become aligned with the company's great vision to leave a positive impact on society and the environment. It was an ambitious goal. She also mandated the removal of aspartame from Diet Pepsi. In addition to a new health-conscious approach, she reevaluated PepsiCo's impact on the environment and focused on several sustainability initiatives to reduce waste, conserve water, and use renewable energy. By 2020, PepsiCo reported using 100 percent renewable electricity. These goals alone were monumental and required serious strategic and tactical approaches to see to fruition. More important, they required the right talent.

Indra partnered with her CHRO and other leaders in her organization to execute the third component to her Performance with a Purpose—creating a culture of employee retention and connection. Indra was intimately involved in the initiatives.

When Doug interviewed her in December 2021, he asked her about her approach to managing and empowering her employees. She said, "We had to remake an already great company and make it even greater from a people management perspective. Performance was performance. We were always going to be a great performing company because that's PepsiCo. But if we were going to perform, and at the same time transform the portfolio, we needed to focus on the environment and cherish our people."[1]

While Indra's big-picture strategy was a primary objective, she didn't sacrifice short-term initiatives for long-term ones. She said, "We can focus on the short term and the long term, provided we judiciously balance that. But, most importantly, I believe in running the company *for the duration of the company*. Leaders don't run it for the duration of five or six years. A company goes on forever." She was reminded of the poem "The Brook" by Alfred Lord Tennyson: "Men may come and men may go, but I go on forever." In other words, she added, "Leaders may come and leaders may go, but companies should last forever." That is not to say, however, that they shouldn't renew themselves and adapt to the times. She continued, "That was the philosophy that I adopted. I thought Performance with Purpose was the way you keep renewing the company with a deep sense of purpose, which can change because the components of purpose can change over time. But the feeling of purpose has to stay deep in your heart."

With the purpose of heart, Indra built a team that complemented her strengths and weaknesses. "I wanted very strong personnel because

I felt they ought to tell me if I was doing something that wasn't quite right. I needed them to be up front because sometimes I can be intimidating. I wanted my head of HR to not only support me, but [also] to challenge me."

Indra asked Cynthia Trudell, who was a retired chief operating officer and a board member at PepsiCo, to become her head of Worldwide HR. Cynthia had urged Indra to examine her organizational structure if she wanted to remain committed to retention. Cynthia understood that people are the most important asset in their companies, and so they needed to be committed to that resource.

One way the two worked together as strategic partners was to focus on the recruitment and training of managers. As we have found in our own research, people leave bosses, not employers. Getting the right people to manage others would be key to PepsiCo fulfilling its ultimate mission. Together they instituted programs for training the managers, including those on how to set objectives and how to give feedback. "I think, at the core, people just want to have a fair shot at their job. They want to be told what to do. They want to do a damned good job. They want to be rewarded at the end of the day for doing a good job and be told what they need to do better the next day so that they can improve." In her own words, she believes in what she calls "the core goodness of people." But she also knows that core goodness needs to be supported, and so every new manager goes through what she calls a management boot camp, so they can better give feedback, as well as align individual goals with company goals and the overall strategic mission. So, in other words, she focused on the fundamentals without losing the big picture.

Everyone Wins

Ultimately, the purpose of aligning the tactical initiatives with the big goals is so that everyone wins. When Phil Jackson asked for each member to, more or less, ask, "What can your team do for you, but what can you do for your team?" he wasn't asking them to compromise their individual achievements for the sake of the big picture. He was saying, in his Zen-like way, that when the whole wins, everyone wins. And he wasn't wrong. Remember when Jackson asked Jordan, "Do you want an MVP or a championship ring?" Jordan thought it was an all-or-nothing ask. Perhaps he recoiled at the questions because he thought he would have to give up his MVP for the sake of the big win. The truth is, the Bulls went on to win six championships, and Jordan went on to win five MVP awards. He was able to accomplish *both*.

The best places to work are those that do both as well. For those companies, where the organization succeeds, so do individuals.

Reinvention Is Key

Colgate-Palmolive is an American icon, one of the oldest, most storied companies in the United States, a multinational consumer-products company that specializes in the distribution of household, health-care, personal-care, and veterinary products. Founded by William Colgate in 1806 as William Colgate & Company, it began as a starch, soap, and candle factory in New York City. By 1873 it had introduced its toothpaste in a jar, and within twenty years it reinvented the way people used toothpaste with the creation of the Colgate Ribbon Dental Cream—that is, the tube of toothpaste. The rest is history.

Twenty-five years later, B. J. Johnson Company, working on its inventions in Milwaukee, Wisconsin, produced a new soap detergent from palm and olive oils—Palmolive, which quickly became the world's most famous dish soap. The two companies joined forces in 1928 and, for the past hundred years or so, have been one of the world's leading consumer package-goods companies.

Whereas having an iconic name and presence in the marketplace has advantages, it also comes with challenges. One common challenge we see is that companies like Colgate-Palmolive are steeped in tradition. They are successful for a reason, having done what worked in the past and having a proven track record in the industry. The challenge is, how does the company continually stay relevant and compete in the talent marketplace as times, needs, and generations change and new companies, starting from scratch, do not have to deal with the same legacy issues?

From its inception, Colgate-Palmolive has been built on innovation and reinvention, and executives knew they didn't simply want to digitize an old performance-management process. They had been working with a paper process and wanted to overhaul it while rethinking the entire way they manage performance. When they came to us, they had very clear goals:

- Align people's performance with strategic priorities.
- Provide focus across the organization on being more agile to drive new innovation.
- Support short-term, cross-functional, team-based work.
- Provide continuous results, measurements, and insights.
- Engage and empower employees who want active control over their own work and career paths and want to partner with managers on their development.
- Provide actionable goals and meaningful, ongoing conversations about performance and career pathing.

When Colgate-Palmolive was going through this process, it also happened to be onboarding a new foreign cosmetics company. Colgate-Palmolive focused on one of its biggest challenges—aligning everyone's performance to shared goals and priorities. When working in an organization that has been acquiring organizations since its inception like Colgate-Palmolive, it's common for employees to become siloed and not have a clear vision of what other parts of the organization are doing. As new organizations are acquired and grow, it's also common to see different parts of organizations adopting their own processes. Colgate-Palmolive was no different. No unified process spanned Colgate-Palmolive for resource planning, let alone managing performance. So, from a systems perspective, Colgate-Palmolive had to rethink every aspect. It wasn't just re-creating a digital performance review; it had to consider the unique company culture.

The team needed to understand how the company used its data, specifically how it rated employees. (Historically, companies have used everything from a five-point to a nine-point rating scale.) Colgate-Palmolive felt it needed to move to a smaller-number scale but not eliminate rating scales completely. After working with us, it still wanted to simplify and streamline the process from an employee rating system of one to seven to a more simplified rating system.

Of course, all these changes take a great deal of thought. Executives surveyed many critical areas of the organization and gathered as much information as possible before revamping the entire process. They knew they needed buy-in.

However, unsurprisingly, the leaders proposing the change were met with some resistance. Through the surveys, they discovered that people within the organization felt they couldn't put the resources behind all the change management required to implement their new system. Also, creating "transparent goals for individuals and the organization" was mind-blowing to some. Overall, many in the organization felt such sweeping changes would create more fear than positive outcomes.

As a result, Colgate-Palmolive started with some smaller goals and focused on engagement and adoption of our Betterworks software application, which allowed it to post goals and make them transparent across the organization. When it went live with the new program, instead of every goal being transparent and focusing on alignment right away, goals for individuals defaulted to private. Colgate-Palmolive's initial plan was to motivate people to think about what *performance* means in a continuous environment. *How do I gather feedback? How do I understand that I focus on the right things from a business and development perspective?*

These concepts can be intimidating at first. Colgate-Palmolive's team was extremely thoughtful with the rollout and implementation of the new process. It worked diligently to create an experience that employees would both enjoy and find easy to use. Colgate-Palmolive was emphatic that it wanted the first experience for a user to be positive. It created actionable goals, meaningful conversations about performance, and career pathing and provided training to engage employees to use their new program. Above all, it empowered the employees to use the program in a way that gave them active control over their own work, career paths, and partnering with their managers on their development.

Helping People through Resistance to Change

Since implementing these changes, Colgate-Palmolive has seen positive outcomes. However, it faces a common challenge that many companies face when switching from a nontransparent, closed process between a manager and an employee. To no one's shock, many employees still feel uncomfortable publicly sharing their individual goals. Although the data shows that visible feedback and goals can be powerful and transformational, Colgate-Palmolive and many companies like them still choose to keep all feedback anonymous and goals private at first. That's appropriate; when rolling out a new process, it's always best to take it slowly. Not everyone will be ready to publicly share their goals or receive feedback in a shared forum. The key when transitioning a company to a new process, specifically goal sharing and feedback, is to create it as nonthreatening as possible. Not everyone is ready for radical changes, especially if this is "how we've been doing it" for nearly one hundred years.

Let's face it, change is hard. People need to see a real benefit to learning how to do something new. They also need accountability and to advocate for themselves. Most employees don't feel their managers advocate for them or have their back. When we empower employees to raise their hands and say, "I want to do more! I want to be challenged more! I want to participate in this goal!" they become invested in the process. When they do so publicly on a lightweight, easy-to-use application that takes little time, we start to see a shift. When people begin to see that they are accomplishing goals, getting feedback on those goals instantly, and not having to wait for an annual performance review, they start to want to participate.

Getting People on Board

We see the implementation of the new process as a complete company-wide change, with strong support for the leaders of the company communicating why they are moving to a new process and what they hope to achieve from inaugurating the application. We recommend inviting people to participate, rather than mandating participation. For the goal-setting process, you can ask people to participate vs. make it mandatory, but of course, for the new performance process of continual conversation, that needs to be implemented company-wide, so you aren't running multiple performance processes simultaneously. And as with any change of mindset and behavior, one must be *willing* to make the change. So, when you're *asking* employees to make a change, they're not *choosing* to do it. It feels like they're being demanded to do it. This can create resistance.

Our philosophy is simple: Let's enable people to volunteer to try this out. We encourage leaders to do it first. So, they can ask their employees to join them. Ultimately, it creates vulnerability. If Doug, as the CEO, and Jamie, as an HR executive, start publishing their goals publicly and giving feedback to each other in real time, employees will see that we are willing to make the changes. They'll also begin to see us make mistakes too. They'll notice that we need help navigating obstacles as well and need help from team members. And when we've had some wins, they'll see those too.

An employee may wonder, *If I do this, will others judge me for messing up? Or worse, will I be fired or disciplined? How am I doing compared to my neighbor? Are they doing more? Are they doing better than me?* These are natural responses to moving a private annual goal-setting process into a public space. It takes a complete cultural, behavioral, and mindset shift. That leads to the ultimate question every organization has to wrestle with at some point: How do we deal with failure and setbacks? If you're a punitive company, it will be difficult for employees to feel safe enough to engage continuously without fear of retribution.

When people are stressed, burned out, or distracted, they tend to fall into old patterns and routines. How does a company avoid this altogether when implementing continuous feedback? By removing the old process and routine. Start fresh and stay consistent, even if it is uncomfortable at first. It's best to take it slowly and thoughtfully, as Colgate-Palmolive did. It's also important to remember that people support what they help create. When they are part of the process and their opinions are valued from the beginning, they will more than likely volunteer and want to participate.

Key Takeaways

- The best way to recruit and retain great talent who would be prepared for this changing landscape is to develop a company's leaders.
- Changing an annual performance review doesn't mean digitizing. It means rethinking and redefining the experience.
- The key when transitioning a company to a new process, specifically goal-sharing and feedback, is to create it as nonthreatening as possible. Not everyone is ready for radical changes, especially if this is "how we've been doing it" for nearly one hundred years.
- The implementation of the new process should be done with strong support for the leaders of the company communicating why they are moving to a new process and shouldn't mandate participation, but rather invite people.
- The best way to get performance-management (what we call performance-enablement) systems to work is to create a culture where honest feedback can be given in a safe environment where employees won't feel threatened.

CHAPTER 7

Scaling Your Initiative with Technology

The Dawn of the Age of Usability

An old quote is falsely attributed to Henry Ford: "If I had asked my customers what they wanted, they would have said a faster horse."[1] What is true is that innovators have for centuries squabbled about the notion that people don't know what they want until they have seen it.

Steve Jobs was a notorious objector to the idea that customers knew what they wanted. If he had limited his vision to simply what people were looking for in the moment, he could not have possibly designed something as sleek, user-friendly, and all-encompassing utilitarian as an iPhone.

Who can forget Steve Jobs's revolutionary introduction of the iPhone in 2007? Standing before a rapt crowd in his signature black turtleneck, dad jeans, and sneakers, he walked the audience through the features of his new creation: "It's an iPod, it's a phone, it's an internet communicator."

As people clapped, hooted, and hollered, he repeated himself and clarified, "This is not three separate devices. This is one device." People couldn't quite comprehend it at first: A handheld computer? A phone? A place to listen to all our music—all in one? A seamless interface? What? Jobs then said, "We're going to reinvent the phone, and here it is." On the screen behind him, he showed a picture of an iPod, with an old rotary dial. The nerds in the crowd gave him a lot of laughs over that one. But, in truth, he wasn't too far off.

He then blasted pictures of the Nokia and Blackberry phones, with their cumbersome keyboards, and explained how these "smartphones" were neither smart, lightweight, nor easy to use. People had already been thinking of integrating phones and computers. Apple wasn't the first. But what Jobs and his team had created revolutionized how this was done—not just what it would look like but also how it functioned. He took a human-centered and design-thinking approach to the product. He observed how people interacted and used their phones, iPods, and computers and made a device that responded to their needs. Stylus? Who needs a stylus or a pointer? He "pointed out" that the best pointers humans have are their own fingers. He then showed a sleek screen where the users could point to what application they wanted, and, voilà, it was there! They could do it all and then slip it right in their pocket. *It's an iPod, a phone, a computer.*

We've come a long way since 2007. It's hard to believe that the teenagers using the iPhones today weren't even born when Steve Jobs introduced it. An entire generation of the population has never known a time when we carried around a laptop, a phone, and an iPod in our messenger bags on the way to work.

As the consumer digital experience was transformed entirely by the iPhone, our expectations for ease of use, convenience, and ongoing optimization—a consumer-grade experience—have extended to the workplace. Driven by the melding of home and office over the last few years, the digital applications and platforms we use to work on have taken on a new significance. They're our window to our world of work—how we connect with our colleagues, managers, customers, and partners.

Despite this, it's stunning to us that so many organizations continue to rely on inelegant systems to run business-critical processes that weren't purpose-built for the heavy lifting required of them. Too many times, we've seen organizations attempt to force fit software that isn't optimized for the task at hand—in an effort, perhaps, to reduce costs or avoid change management—which results in an overall lackluster employee experience at best and a frustrating, disengaging one at worst.

Organizations serious about evolving their performance-management practices need a technological solution built for the purpose. To successfully transition to performance enablement, they need an iPhone, not a Nokia, a tool that does things for them they haven't yet even dreamed of.

The Fitbit for Business

In 2013 a team committed to developing and shepherding a new philosophy of work built around the OKR methodology of goal-setting met to form Betterworks. Its mission was to help businesses all over the world develop high-performing teams by leveraging the same goal-setting process that Intel, Google, and other inspiring companies relied on in their early years to achieve hypergrowth and market dominance in their respective industries. Since Betterworks's founding, companies have had 2,103,884 (and counting) goals completed using our technology and have facilitated over 1,227,427 manager-employee conversations. Employees who use our software average about 84,000 updates per week (which translates to about once every seven days for each employee), communicating to their teams their work progress or roadblocks and cheering and nudging one another as they reach key milestones.

The notion behind the company came from a group of creators that wanted an application that functioned something like a Fitbit for business. They wanted to see a snapshot of company progress at any point: How many proverbial steps (goals) did we take today? Where are we stalled out or not progressing as well? What's our pulse—how many conversations are our managers and leaders having? Is everyone moving in the same direction?

What they ultimately envisioned was a continuous feedback mechanism for business that provided visibility into company performance, from collective progress toward the highest-level strategic objectives, down to the individual employee's achievements. They wanted this picture in real time, so they could see what was going on as it was unfolding, versus looking back to see what had happened. And they wanted to be able to do this every day, not just once or twice a year.

When our company was developing, we were fortunate to have John Doerr as an early investor. John worked for Andy Grove, the father of OKRs, who, as the CEO at a pivotal inflection point in the company's history, used them to help run Intel and ultimately win the microprocessor war. After John left Intel, he became a partner at Kleiner Perkins, introducing the concept of OKRs to every single portfolio company he invested in. John was an early investor in companies like Google, Amazon, and Intuit, all of which he advised to use some version of OKRs in their operations. Google, for example, was using OKRs when it had fifteen people inside the organization. Today, they have 175,000, and they still use OKRs as a means to align and measure company performance.

A few years into the development of our platform, our team realized that OKRs by themselves can sometimes feel a lot like a tax to the individual contributor. *Why can't I just do my work? Why do I have to report on my work? And why do I have to update my goals and explain how I'm doing against them?* We found that it was critical to add a component of conversation and employee engagement around those goals—and not just for employee satisfaction but also because it improves outcomes.

At this time, Betterworks had its own iPhone moment: What if instead of simply being the place where goals were documented, tracked, and measured, it became the place where managers and employees regularly connected and where end-to-end company and employee performance were managed, measured, and enabled?

As someone who had deep experience in the HR software space, Doug came on board to help realize this vision. He believed that adding the other proven elements of performance support—conversations (or check-ins), recognition, and feedback—to the platform would be key. Instead of feeling like a tax, we wanted it to feel like a benefit: How could an individual employee be made better by the process? How could their career improve even beyond this role? Could it enable them to feel like they are contributing to the company as a whole and that the work they do matters? And most important, how could we extend this model of performance enablement, underpinned by goal-setting and conversations, to manage those goals and improve the annual review process, turning it into something employees embrace and truly moves the needle on performance?

As our technology has evolved to help make work better for hundreds of thousands of employees in the years since Betterworks's inception, our understanding of what a platform must provide to comprehensively enable performance across an organization has evolved with it. In addition to the core capabilities we've established to this point, there are other features we believe the best organizations provide to their people to help them reach their full potential.

Rounding Out the Modern Performance-Enablement Platform

Traditional performance management—and therefore the decisions that result from it—is highly prone to normal human biases. Removing these biases should be a primary goal of any performance-management process and system. Unfair biases and inconsistent ratings put certain individuals at a disadvantage and cause employees to leave your organization. That is why the performance-calibration process was introduced, through which managers discuss their proposed employee ratings with other managers to agree on a common criterion against which their direct reports will be rated. The goal is to find common ground that makes consistent employee-performance evaluations possible. Unfortunately, the traditional, manual calibration process is far from perfect, requiring significant preparation time from both managers and HR—and it may *still* be biased because it could be heavily influenced by the best debater in the room.

Betterworks's calibration capability simplifies and enriches the traditional calibration process, allowing for much lighter process overhead and better talent decisions. First, it makes key performance data—including the employee's goal achievement, development feedback, and recognition—easily visible to managers during calibration to avoid manager bias and recency bias.

Leaders are able to easily compare employee groups using filters such as location, gender, ethnicity, age, and more to uncover any unequal treatment. With this, Betterworks calibration helps companies fulfill their commitment to diversity, equity, and inclusion (DE&I) by alerting managers to any hidden biases among specific groups. With just a few clicks, managers can gather objective performance insights and see whether decisions are impacting certain employee populations unfairly. This data makes a difference—creating a foundation of transparency and trust between employees, HR, managers, and the review process as a whole. This all helps in the calibration process when it comes time to promote or develop an employee or transition them out of the company.

HR, Executive, and Manager Insights

One of the key benefits of moving away from traditional performance processes and toward a continuous model of performance enablement is the rich data and insight into your workforce that it yields. With performance data points across the whole of an employee's tenure, leaders are equipped to make much more accurate and data-driven decisions than if they were solely relying on a once- or twice-a-year conversation.

The Business Leader's People Performance Dashboard

The executive can gather the following insights:

- With regard to goal progress, where in my team are things stuck? Where can I help unblock them?
- I can show that I care by taking quick action. I identify whom to cheer, whom to nudge, where to comment, and how to best support and encourage teams, managers, and individuals.

The Cockpit for Team Managers

The manager can glean these insights:

- I can be on top of things: What are the performance best practices when my team is doing well? Doing less well? What should I prioritize? How can I reinforce best practices?
- I coach more accurately: Whom should I have which discussion with? Who hasn't set personal goals yet? Who has

received constructive feedback about certain competencies that should be included in a development plan?

- To help the team on the fly, I can request feedback and recognition from others on cross-functional teams.

The Command Center for HR

HR professionals can access these insights:

- I can gauge program health. I know where to provide support or guidance by viewing heat maps of the organization in terms of goal-setting, conversation completion, and feedback given and received—all grouped by department or manager.
- To uncover insights for leadership, I see distribution analysis of conversation answers and identify the percentage of top potential employees deemed at risk of leaving, and I identify interventions.

Employee Engagement Surveys

Employees are a company's most valuable asset, and their engagement—defined as the strength of the mental and emotional connection employees feel toward the work they do, their teams, and their organization—is vital to business success. Studies verify that highly engaged organizations see increased profitability. One meta-analysis from Gallup found that employee engagement is responsible for decreased absenteeism by 81 percent, turnover by 18 percent, and product defects by 41 percent and, on the flip side, increased customer satisfaction by 10 percent and profitability by as much as 23 percent in top-quartile engagement companies compared to bottom-quartile engagement companies. Engagement surveys are a foundational tool for listening to employees and assessing where and how improvements can be prescribed, in turn improving business outcomes.

Engagement surveys alone, however, do not initiate change or action. Therefore, action planning and implementation must be incorporated into an engagement-survey process.

Before collecting survey responses, analyzing results, and supporting action, effective engagement-survey processes start with technology capable of reaching all employees. A common roadblock to surveying employees is that survey tools are not able to capture all employee population data—including all traditional and nontraditional employees who might not have a corporate email or access to all company programs.

Deep Integration with Key Business Systems

To build on our earlier discussion of the importance of integrations in ensuring a seamless employee experience, we'll now explore two key categories of integrations critical to ensuring that your performance processes are connected to other core HR functions.

Integration with HCM Systems

HCM (human capital management) systems provide a wide range of HR and workforce-management functionality, offering companies a single source of truth for employee data and a single application for administration, talent, recruiting, benefits, payroll, and more. But when it comes to inspiring, engaging, and guiding employee performance, these systems fall short. That's because huge HCM tools are burdensome to access on a daily basis and not intuitive, specific, or engaging enough to become a habit in anyone's work life.

Lack of adoption has the spiraling effect of reducing the quality of information until such systems are all but unusable—performance reviews are based on neglected, outdated goals, and insights into goals are stale. Everyone becomes frustrated—employees, managers, and HR—and the system loses credibility. As we like to say, we make these HCM solutions better by giving them a performance process that's new and current and seen as valuable by the managers and individual contributors.

Integration with Learning Management Systems (LMS)

Many studies have shown that the majority of employees and managers at most companies feel their company's training programs do not measurably improve business performance, and most companies don't even bother to track the returns they get on their investments in training. This is because learning and performance are not integrated. By integrating these core processes, organizations can see the impacts learning programs have on employee performance and, eventually, on business outcomes.

When employees create business or professional-development goals in Betterworks, they can associate them with LinkedIn Learning or a Udemy course. When the employee makes progress on courses, their goal progress in Betterworks is automatically updated in real time. Managers have instant visibility into an employee's learning progress and thus have more context for coaching and developing their team members. They can make sure team members make time to progress in, and eventually complete, the courses. They can discuss with them new projects to apply their newly learned skills to, improving learning retention and providing opportunities for the employee to stretch him- or herself.

Key Takeaways

- Effective performance technology needs to support a dynamic workforce and workplace, incorporate accessibility as a core design principle, comply with local and international regulations, integrate with existing and future investments, and keep data safe.

- Frequent, relevant feedback coupled with *personal recognition* has the power to transform employee performance and culture. Recognition promotes teamwork, collaboration, and cultural values—and you can amplify that impact by making appreciation visible company-wide.

- One of the best ways to ensure you're enabling performance is to use an enterprise software program that increases engagement, is lightweight, and allows for bidirectional feedback between employees and managers.

CHAPTER 8

Compensation

IN 2018, AT the Women in the World Summit, Viola Davis, star of the movies *Fences*, *The Help*, *Widows*, and *Doubt*, sat with Tina Brown for an interview and discussed the pay gap in Hollywood. At the time, it didn't make too much of a stir. But when the video of the interview resurfaced in 2020 during the height of the pandemic, when people were struggling with working from home and added pressure, not to mention homeschooling, it went viral. It also sparked a more significant debate about what it means to pay for performance.

Davis argued in the clip, "I got the Oscar. I got the Emmy. I got the two Tonys. I've done Broadway. I've done TV. I've done film. I've done all of it. I have a career that's probably comparable to Meryl Streep, Julianne Moore, and Sigourney Weaver. They all came out of Yale, they came out of Julliard, they came out of NYU. They had the same path as me, and yet I am nowhere near them, not as far as money, not as far as job opportunities, nowhere close to it. But I have to constantly get on that phone . . . and people say: 'You're a Black Meryl Streep. . . . There is no one like you.' Okay, then if there's no one like me, you think I'm that, then you pay me what I'm worth. You give me what I'm worth."[1] She was clearly, and justly, upset that she is not being compensated appropriately for her level of performance.

She is just as qualified, learned, and accomplished as many of her higher-paid contemporaries.

Many people took to social media to commiserate with Davis when this clip resurfaced. Though they didn't have her credentials or awards, they felt something was inherently unjust about how they were paid. Davis's cry to "pay me what I'm worth" resonated deeply with people from all genders, races, and socioeconomic classes, even though Davis made the compelling case that her lack of pay was indeed because of her particular gender and race. According to the National Women's Law Center, women in the United States who work full-time year-round are paid only eighty-four cents for every dollar paid to men. Black women have to work up to August 22 of the following calendar year to earn as much as their white male counterparts do in a year. Overall, women of every race are paid less than men at all education levels, which worsens as women's careers progress.[2]

Davis's interview forced the more central questions facing all employers: How do you measure someone's worth? How do you decide how much to pay for someone's performance? How do you accurately value work and performance? And when is the best time to do that?

Granted, not all employees are performing on the world stage as Davis is. Still, many are performing in their workplace and wondering, *How can my employers even make this determination?* Of course, we believe race and gender should never be determinants when measuring performance. But even without gender or race as an issue, determining pay and what someone is worth is quite complex, and there is no one-size-fits-all solution. However, one way to improve the process is by decoupling compensation from annual performance reviews.

Establishing the willingness to take annual performance reviews out of the compensation conversation is a significant obstacle for most employers to overcome when deciding whether to shift to our software. Many companies tell us they cannot switch from their current performance-management software because their compensation is tied directly to annual reviews. After all, annual reviews are where employers determine their employees' ratings, which are used to identify the people to promote, maintain, or manage, in addition to how much to compensate them. However, we strongly feel this excuse is deeply flawed and only holding companies back—for several reasons:

- The world's moved away from ratings. We can't put people into classes. It's demotivating to the seventy percent of the employees lumped in the mediocre box, and, as we've pointed out, ratings are not always accurate.
- Connecting yearly ratings to compensation places an unnecessary Herculean burden on HR managers and leaders to conduct performance reviews, calibrate ratings, and promote and manage pay increases all at once.
- Because of the unnecessary burden, many HR leaders have moved the compensation-review process out six months. They're basically using six-month-old data to make compensation decisions. The world changes quickly. Companies are scrambling to meet the demands of inflation, competitive markets, and industry downturns and upswings that don't care what time of year it is.
- New laws demanding transparency of salary and pay scales (such as the ones taking effect in New York and California) are changing employees' expectations. For example, employees

can see what their company's competitors are offering and what their colleagues in the same company earn. Salary transparency changes the game. Organizations that want to remain competitive and retain top talent will need to be agile and flexible, which includes compensation.

A Complex Issue Demands a Reimagined Strategy

On the heels of the pandemic and the Great Resignation, we're now facing an unprecedented rate of inflation and, as a result, labor challenges. And one of the most critical issues facing employees right now is compensation. With inflation around 6.5 percent as of January 2023, many employees demand that their pay be commensurate with their experience and performance, not to mention the increased cost of living. According to Payscale's *2022 Compensation Best Practices Report*, 44 percent of organizations say that pay is why they lose top talent.[3] Companies that are more agile and responsive and able to offer increases throughout the year and not just annually have a much better shot at retaining top talent than those that wait a whole year to offer raises.

We've also found that the best compensation strategies cover the big picture, beyond just performance, ratings, and pay. An excellent compensation strategy considers current industry demands, the economy, and the needs of their employees, such as the desire for remote work, flexibility, mental and physical health support, vacation time, and stock options. For example, an employer might review compensation the second week of each quarter, or include rotating functions, such as looking at engineering the second week of March and the accounting department the second week of June. A strategy might be to periodically examine how long it's been since employees had a compensation increase. You could look at it from a financial perspective: "This is the sum of money we want to use for compensation increases each quarter, and this is how we want to divide it among departments." If you break it down throughout the year, it's not a massive process for the company all at once.

Many companies struggle to adapt to the hybrid and work-from-home models, not to mention to figurie out how to adjust compensation for those that work in the office versus those that work from home. Do companies need to adjust based on where employees work? For example, does someone who works remotely in a small Midwestern town still receive a salary comparable to that of New York City peers? Does it matter? Should it matter? The answers aren't simple, and organizations must respond in the moment, especially when attracting top talent.

Of course, a great compensation strategy focuses on equity. Most organizations take this seriously, especially in the wake of the #MeToo movement, which exposed widespread harassment and discrimination in the workplace. What's encouraging is that only 9 percent of organizations surveyed in Payscale's *2022 Compensation Best Practices Report* said that they wouldn't do pay equity analysis in their companies because "leadership believes the pay gaps are nonsense."[4] That means most companies who participated in the survey were taking pay equity seriously. According to the same study, 66 percent of companies said they had already planned initiatives, and 38 said they are doing something to address pay gaps they are already aware of.[5]

Transparency is also crucial when rethinking your compensation strategy. Love it or hate it, the world as we know it emphasizes transparency. The trend is not going away. We know there was a time when speaking about salaries was taboo, and salary ranges were rarely even listed in job advertisements. But generational shifts have demanded a fresh look at how companies discuss salaries and compensation. Unlike boomers, Gen Xers, millennials, and Gen Zers are comfortable sharing their lives in public. With shifts to payment apps like Venmo, people even share who they are paying and for what. All their followers and connections can see they split a pizza with friends last night. Nothing is a secret anymore. Unsurprisingly, younger generations do not to think twice about talking openly about their salaries. If leaders believe that employees aren't sharing their salary information with their peers, they live in a fantasy world. Ultimately, the best compensation strategy is one that reimagines how, when, and why compensation is adjusted, apart from annual performance reviews.

The Case for Decoupling Employee Compensation from Annual Performance Reviews[6]

Despite what the old guard may think about not being able to change the performance-review process, we think you can. Before we tell you how, we believe it is essential to dig a little deeper into compensation, including using it as a motivator for performance. Davis's appeal to "pay me what I'm worth" implies that she is only motivated by the pay. But there is much more to pay and compensation than money alone. Increased job opportunities, meaningful work, and accolades and recognition also count as compensation. Tied up in Davis's conversation with Tina Brown, but not explicitly said, is the notion that Viola wanted to be *recognized for her worth*—her humanity, dignity, work, time, and abilities. Her appeal goes much deeper than pay.

For years, HR leaders, managers, and CEOs have been working together to figure out more nuanced approaches to motivating performance. However, before one rethinks performance-based pay, it's essential to understand how compensation influences employee performance. Although it may encourage employees to perform in some measure, merit-based pay also introduces some risks, such as the following.

Monetary Rewards May Incentivize the Wrong Outcomes

Employees may prioritize the wrong aspects of performance when incentivized only by money. For example, they may cut corners on quality to meet a quota or use unethical practices, such as opening fraudulent accounts to satisfy goal requirements. There is no shortage of examples, but one of the most infamous is the well-documented Wells Fargo case. Under pressure to meet quotas for performance-based pay, bank employees opened millions of savings and checking accounts in the names of actual customers. None of the customers, mostly elderly individuals, consented to having their names used, much less to opening the accounts. This fraudulent behavior went on for decades. Finally, after numerous lawsuits, Wells Fargo agreed to pay $3 billion in fines to settle a civil lawsuit and resolve the criminal case.

Although these circumstances are extreme, they nevertheless show that monetary rewards can dilute the quality of work and can lead to employees making poor decisions instead of decisions aligned with their company's values. Sometimes it can cost companies billions by putting the wrong performance metrics in place.

Doug once knew a leader of a professional services team who incentivized the team by saying, "If you can deliver your projects in under forty hours, we will give you a bonus." It didn't take long for employees to figure out how to game the system. Upon review, leadership discovered that these projects actually required upward of 120 hours to complete! The employees were delivering the projects in full—meaning they weren't cutting corners. Rather, they were lying about how long it took them so they could collect their bonuses. That meant the company wasn't able to bill the client for the full 120 hours of work (extra hours) *and* it had to pay bonuses. Needless to say, the company lost millions of dollars. Unwittingly, this leader incentivized his employees to lie, which often happens when the wrong performance metrics are in place.

Also worth considering is that if employees are focused only on getting the work done to collect a paycheck and leave, they may lose sight of the greater purpose of their work. That loss of focus can pull them out of the organizational culture and lead to disengagement over time.

Performance-Based Pay Magnifies Bias and Inequity

Performance-based compensation can get muddled easily, potentially magnifying existing unconscious biases. Performance management has traditionally been subject to many biases. What follows is an exhaustive, but by no means complete, list created by Bold Culture, a global, data-driven, multicultural communication and management consulting firm.

Affinity bias occurs when people tend to connect or bond with people who share similar backgrounds, experiences, and interests. Sometimes saying someone isn't a "culture fit" is masking an affinity bias. Someone with that bias might say, "Bob is too introverted. He keeps to himself and likes to read in his spare time. He wouldn't fit in here, because we're a group of extroverted and outgoing individuals who like to spend time together after hours."

Age bias happens when we penalize someone based on age. This doesn't just mean being biased against older people; it applies to any age. Examples of bias include saying "millennials are whiners" or "boomers are out of touch." Sometimes it's much more subtle: "We need more energy [or new blood] around here." Sometimes it manifests as different treatment or making assumptions, such as that older workers won't adapt to new technology or social media.

Conformity bias means "peer pressure." We all have the desire to belong; at times we can feel pressured to go along with peers or senior employees, regardless of our own beliefs or ideas. A common example of conformity bias is when a senior manager loves a candidate and gets others to agree, not based on the candidate's credentials but on the team members' desire to please their manager.

Anchoring bias is also known as the expectation bias, which occurs when someone holds on to a piece of information to make a decision. For example, a qualified person applying for a position has a low salary requirement. The hiring manager can then view all other applicants who ask for more as unsuitable or asking for too much.

Attribution bias, a.k.a. first-impression bias, happens when you assess or judge another based on a first or prior interaction. This bias can often cause managers to dismiss someone or even highly rate someone based on early interactions rather than on the full scope of the person's performance. For example, you could have a wonderful first meeting with a person that colors all your future interactions. That employee could be a poor performer, but because you had one early positive interaction you refuse to see it. The same goes for a negative first impression. No matter what the person does after, you may still see the employee in a negative light.

Confirmation bias is the inclination to draw conclusions about a situation or person based on your personal desires, beliefs, and prejudices rather than on unbiased merit. A person who is a Stanford or

Harvard alum can assume that because another graduate from the same university has the same credentials he or she is more qualified than someone who attended another school.

Contrast bias is the comparison of two or more things that you have come into contact with—either simultaneously or one after another—causing you to exaggerate the performance of one in contrast to the other. For example, you might judge an employee based on another employee's performance, rather than the first employee's job description or the company's standard.

Excessive leniency (and its opposite, **severity bias**) from the manager can adversely affect employees' ratings or mobility in a company. For example, one manager can be too kind or lenient, and another can be hardened and tough. We've all had schoolteachers who all but guaranteed us an A, and then we learned to avoid the old battle axes. Word would spread quickly that the latter teachers were not to be messed with—no second chances, no test makeups, no grading on the curve. Similarly, excessively lenient leaders don't put their foot down: "Late to work again? No problem!" "Missed a deadline? You'll meet the next one!" "Keep falling asleep in meetings? Go home early. You obviously need some rest." Other managers stand by the door to ensure you're there on time. They hover over you while you work or discredit your work. When it's time to give ratings, they hesitate to dole out praise.

Fundamental attribution bias refers to an individual's tendency to attribute another's actions to their character or personality while attributing their own behavior to external situational factors outside their control. For example, a manager may call someone "lazy," "not detail-oriented," or a "poor writer" for missing typos but may miss typos or have lapses him- or herself.

Horn or halo bias occurs when the worker's performance is appraised solely based on a perceived negative or positive quality. The term *halo effect* was first used in the 1920s by Edward Thorndike, an American psychologist who noted that attractive people tend to be perceived as competent and successful. These usually charming, good-looking angels can get away with things that an unattractive person might not be able to—such as poor communication, performance, or behavior. A study by Kelton Research found that "when looking at images, Americans perceive those with straight teeth to be 45% more likely than those with crooked teeth to get a job when competing with someone who has a similar skill set and experience. They are also seen as 58% more likely to be successful."[7] Someone's teeth or smile shouldn't determine employability or ability to perform. Yet, it is very much an unconscious determinant.

As you might guess, the horn effect is the opposite; it deals with immediately attributing negative qualities to someone based on an aspect of the person's appearance or character. For example, if a person appears to be out of shape, it might be assumed that the person doesn't take care of him- or herself or is lazy. Likewise, hair color, tattoos, and fashion preferences can all trigger unconscious bias and cause people to be perceived inaccurately.

Nonverbal bias happens when analyzing nonverbal communication attributes such as body language or eye contact when making a decision. For example, you might assume someone who doesn't make eye contact when speaking is lying, without having any evidence. Similarly, a person can be very charming, shake hands firmly, make eye contact, and mirror your physical actions in order to establish trust while in reality they may be lying.

Recency bias describes recent trends or behavior patterns overshadowing past actions. That means someone who performed excellently in the fourth quarter but rested on laurels while leaving work to their team members earlier in the year could be rewarded because the recent performance is top of mind for the manager. Conversely, a consistent high performer could have a bad month, week, or day, which can loom large in the psyche of the manager and not accurately reflect the employee's overall performance.

Sexual identity, race, gender, and religion biases are serious, and most organizations have systems supporting diversity, inclusion, and equity. However, that doesn't mean that these types of discrimination don't happen. Whether they want to admit it or not, all people have some form of unconscious bias. Even the best managers do.

Stereotyping is the most common form of bias—it happens when people assign a set of characteristics to all members of a group and ignore individual attributes, experiences, or characteristics.

In addition to these biases, whether an employee has met goals and earned a monetary reward on a merit-based pay system is often left to the manager's discretion. As a result, there's a greater risk of managers favoring employees they're closer to or whom they see more often. As more companies adopt long-term hybrid work, this bias becomes even more challenging to control.

Merit-Based Pay Doesn't Make Employees Work Harder

Yes, monetary rewards are an extrinsic motivator. People work to make money—they may have families to feed, roofs to keep over their heads, school loans to pay back, and lifestyles they have become accustomed to. However, most employees can work anywhere if money is the only incentive. That is to say, money alone doesn't drive people to work. People choose careers and paths for a variety of reasons. Earning money is only one of them. People have interests, talents, and passions, and they usually pick careers that reflect them. Money alone rarely incentivizes employees to work harder or become more engaged in their work. Performance-based pay doesn't connect the employee with the greater organization or culture. That motivator is more transactional and less aspirational than intrinsic motivators.

You need employees to find their rewards in work itself. Whether a desire to be an active participant in workplace culture or a desire to find learning opportunities embedded within daily tasks, an intrinsic motivator drives more significant performance potential than monetary rewards.

Other than Pay, What *Does* Motivate Employees?

Our philosophy is that the following intrinsic motivators incentivize better performance.

Meaning and Purpose

A sense of purpose most incentivizes employees in their roles. When they can get past the daily grind and find meaning in their work, they're more likely to aspire to achieve greater things and work harder to get there.

To drive a greater sense of purpose, show employees the entire life-cycle of your company's product. Manufacturing employees, for example, could see the final product. Customer service representatives could see positive NPS scores from happy customers. Seeing what they're contributing to can help employees find their sense of fulfillment in work.

Goal alignment supports meaning and purpose for employees too. When employees can see the strategic value of their work and how it produces business results, they're more likely to find meaning and job satisfaction, leading to better individual performance.

Opportunities for Development, Advancement, and Growth

Employees must see opportunities to develop and reach their full potential within your company. Employees become more driven and find the work more fulfilling when working toward something tangible or meaningful. One way to instill this drive and sense of meaning is by providing clear career paths and options for mobility within the company. In addition, the prospect of promotion can improve employee performance. High-performing employees are more inclined to invest in their future and work hard to achieve their goals.

Connected, Inclusive Culture

Culture is a crucial factor in motivating the behaviors you want to see. When employees feel connected to the business, they'll understand how their work impacts their colleagues. That team spirit drives more significant investment in the support of the culture and can improve individual performance.

A sense of community and culture inspires greater job satisfaction, motivating employees to work harder. But changing norms, like the shift to remote work, complicates your ability to build a connected culture. Tools like goal-alignment software bring employees together to work toward a shared purpose, enabling performance from hybrid teams.

Frequent Feedback and Recognition

Employees need a line of communication with managers to receive feedback and recognition in the flow of work. Frequent feedback helps team members see how they're performing, which can inspire high-performing employees to take greater pride in their work.

Don't underestimate the power of recognition. Performance-based pay is rarely as motivating as frequent feedback and recognition of work well done. Even if it's just oral, receiving recognition from managers can motivate employees to work harder and produce higher-quality work.

Recognition from top leaders can be even more inspiring. Employees want to feel like they're moving in the right direction. There are few more validating and rewarding things than hearing your future plans confirmed by top-level leaders.

How to Get Rid of Annual Performance-Related Compensation

We've found that the best way to keep high-performing employees moving in the right direction is to ditch performance-related pay in favor of performance enablement and employee empowerment. The following discusses ways you can begin to make the shift.

Move from Performance Management to Performance Enablement

The most critical aspect of employee enablement is helping employees see their work's role in driving business results. Connecting employees to the business strategy provides greater intrinsic motivation. When they know what they're working toward, employees can take more control over their work. That sense of autonomy drives greater engagement and job satisfaction—and better performance.

Aligned goals are easier to track and, if written correctly, provide clear performance metrics. The objectives and key results (OKRs) allow employees to set their own goals to drive the business forward.

But determining the key results forces employees to be more thoughtful about performance metrics. Setting performance metrics that produce tangible business results does much more to inspire extraordinary performance than performance-based compensation.

Managers play an essential role in connecting employees to the business. As coaches, managers can help employees gain greater self-awareness, helping them understand their learning opportunities and engage with their roles better. Armed with a clear organizational chart and career paths, managers can help employees discover their options for mobility within the company. In addition, the ability to grow within your organization can help employees harness their potential to perform better.

Employee development is vital for building greater capabilities for your business, and it gives employees something to work toward that they may value more than performance-based pay. Development opportunities demonstrate that the company is invested in the employee's growth and learning.

Performance-based compensation doesn't give employees anything to aspire to beyond rewards. *Performance enablement helps employees see what they're capable of and helps them achieve it.*

Engineer New Incentives

Develop new incentive programs to motivate employee engagement and performance. For example, consider rewarding employees with greater responsibilities, leadership opportunities, or flexible working arrangements.

Some of these incentives, like taking on greater responsibility, may be tied to compensation. But compensation, in this case, isn't the underlying factor motivating employee performance.

You can use several platforms to incentivize performance through nonmonetary rewards, such as experiences employees have always wanted—learning opportunities, vacation, or travel benefits. An engaging rewards program gives employees the freedom to choose their rewards, better motivating each employee to achieve goals.

Reframe Compensation as Total Rewards

McKinsey & Company researchers Sabrin Chowdhury, Neel Gandhi, and Alex Katen-Narvell found that the COVID-19 pandemic led organizations to rethink their total rewards—both financial and nonfinancial. The pandemic forced many people to reevaluate what they truly wanted out of their life and work, leaving unfulfilling jobs and what they deemed toxic cultures that didn't value their health or well-being. As a result, many organizations are rethinking their compensation strategy more holistically. Chowdhury, Gandhi, and Katen-Narvell define total rewards as the "strategy and set of principles that govern these offerings—the 'why' behind the 'what.'" They argue, "Organizations must demonstrate that they have structured their rewards fairly by transparently communicating the link among business performance, individual performance, and rewards."[8]

Their research in transforming major organizations' performance management highlights three guiding principles for designing a total rewards philosophy:

- "Organizations should be clear about what outcomes they want to incentivize."[9] In other words, organizations should set goals frequently and transparently and intentionally incentivize employees—with nonfinancial and financial rewards.

- "Have a clear employee value proposition with differentiated rewards to attract talent and drive performance."[10] Rewards need not be financial—there are many nonfinancial ways to reward employees—flex time, health and wellness benefits, public recognition, and so forth.
- "Segments may require different rewards structures that include agile teams and team-based incentives."[11]

We add that moving to quarterly feedback sessions and calibrations saves time and helps the organization stay agile to pivot when uncontrollable circumstances, such as pandemics, inflation, and economic downturns and upswings occur.

Flexibility can be part of your total rewards strategy. Employees need to achieve an appropriate balance between work and personal life. When you take care of their mental health and give them time to live a complete life outside of work, employees become more loyal and work harder for you.

Consider Variable Pay

In some professions, such as sales or customer success, a percentage of income can be tied to performance—up to as much as 50 percent of total income, in some cases. Although some roles must have commissions or variable incentives in place, best practices suggest confining variable pay only to positions where the outcomes are clearly and completely measurable, such as a dollar-value sales quota. Issues with variable incentives tend to arise when a significant portion of compensation is tied to more qualitative outcomes, such as onboarding a new employee or meeting with a certain number of new prospects, for which measurement isn't as clear-cut.

In addition to commissions, bonuses may also fall under variable pay. Bonuses should be tied to clear metrics using the same criteria as commissions. Not every role may qualify for bonuses, as some outcomes are more challenging to measure than others. Consider which roles qualify for bonuses when setting your compensation strategy.

Communicate Your Strategy to Employees

Employees and management should feel comfortable having open conversations about compensation. Transparency from leadership—especially around hot-button topics like pay—is key to supporting better employee experience and job satisfaction.

If you're no longer relying on performance-related pay to increase your employees' salaries, explain what criteria you're using instead. Help employees understand how rewards are distributed and how pay bands are calculated.

Work to Build a Culture of Transparency around Compensation

Employees should never feel like they can't approach their manager to ask how their pay is being factored or that they can't talk to colleagues about their income. The more open leadership is about to pay, the more transparent the culture. Such transparency has helped employees inside various companies to bring to light pay inequities, assisting organizations to move closer to closing the pay gap.

Redesign Your Compensation Strategy around a Performance-Enablement Plan

Performance-based compensation isn't the only pay strategy out there. You can design a compensation strategy that works for your business and company culture and that doesn't rely on managers interpreting performance to mete out arbitrary monetary rewards. If you're ditching annual review performance-based pay, you need to clarify *what payment is based upon*. We recommend designing a compensation plan that is clear and transparent and can be viewed by everyone in the company.

How to Create a Performance-Enablement Plan

A performance-enablement plan incorporates concrete goals for unleashing an employee's potential. The plans should be aligned with each employee's goals and aspirational goals, or a goal in which 70 percent achievement is adequate. Rather than just offering feedback when performance runs off track, this model encourages managers to function as coaches to keep performance-enablement plans on track. When managers know employee career goals, they can help match employees with learning and experience opportunities to hone desired skills.

Performance-Enablement Plans Require Quarterly Reviews

Performance-enablement plans should coincide with company goals and align employee performance with business results. These plans should be implemented alongside goals on a quarterly basis and close with a quarterly formal review.

Using enterprise-management tools like Betterworks, managers can collect quarterly data on how their reports are progressing toward reaching their potential within the company. Then, at their quarterly review, managers can share this information with their reports. This review process is the only time managers should look backward, and only with the explicit intention of using past performance as a learning opportunity.

A Successful Performance-Enablement Model
That Decouples Compensation from Performance

For the performance-enablement model to be successful, you need a few specific elements that encourage collaboration, communication, and learning. These are the critical elements of a successful performance-enablement model.

Empower the Managers

Managers play the most critical role in performance enablement. Yet, they often receive the least amount of training and guidance to carry out their duties. Managers need to become coaches who can collaborate with employees to identify and remove roadblocks to success.

HR leaders must assess manager roles and adjust managers' priorities to focus less on operational tasks and more on coaching their team members. Your company should also work with learning and development to provide managers with practical scenario-based training designed to hone their coaching skills on an ongoing basis.

Make Learning a Daily Priority

As you shift from performance management to performance enablement, you must embed learning within employee workflows to help managers develop their knowledge and skills throughout the workday. Train managers to communicate the learning opportunities inherent in employees' daily tasks and work experiences. A data-entry task, for example, offers an employee the opportunity to exercise attention to detail. Each employee has a unique learning style, so managers may need to start by introducing more significant concepts and then reinforce those concepts in daily practice.

Clarify Roles and Expectations

Employees need to know what managers expect before they can improve their performance and move forward. Collaborate with managers to clearly define and document goals for every role. When your business sets its quarterly goals, managers and employees should work together to set individual goals aligned with company objectives.

Individual, team, and organizational goals should be updated and communicated as performance expectations and business priorities evolve. In addition, employees should be able to access goals whenever they need to track their progress, adjust their learning goals, or seek specific feedback from their managers.

Use Data to Keep Moving Forward

Although performance isn't usually black and white, managers can leverage performance data points to hold employees accountable and gauge their contributions to overall business objectives. In HR applications there is a significant amount of data—conversational data, feedback data, goal-attainment data—and Betterworks exposes all that data to you so that you can use it not just from a single source but also from multiple points, to help determine an employee's performance. Some companies now use AI to analyze conversation data in real time—such mpathic.ai, which calls itself the "Grammarly of empathy." Its application integrates with platforms for what it calls "on-demand" empathy analysis of both text and voice communications to improve customer service, sales, recruiting, and other public-facing operations.

Managers can also align each employee's goals with the desired business outcome so that employees can see their progress. Performance data serves other crucial purposes, such as helping managers proactively identify skills gaps and learning opportunities, providing personalized coaching, and recognizing team member achievements.

Separate Conversations around Performance and Compensation

After introducing quarterly performance reviews and creating a continuous feedback system, you still need to have conversations around compensation, but they shouldn't be held at the same time. Quarterly check-ins should be a place to establish forward-looking goals. Compensation conversations should be held periodically or as needed. Have the employee's responsibilities increased? Has something else changed? Have needs in the organization changed? Is the employee ready for greater responsibility? Is something happening in the industry? Are your salaries competitive in your field or area?

Implement a Ratingless System

If you are decoupling compensation from annual reviews, how can you calculate compensation? Many companies are adopting what they're calling "ratingless reviews." Because managers and supervisors often don't concentrate on individual performance but rather on ratings, bias is possible. In contrast to ratings, we have found the best way to offset this bias is by having calibration meetings to discuss employees' performances and agree on a uniform way to allocate performance bonuses and pay.

Use Calibration to Improve and Gain Unbiased Data-Driven Insights into Employee Performance and Compensation

Many companies already use some version of the calibration process in their annual reviews. Managers and HR together find common ground to evaluate employees. This practice is designed to limit the biases discussed. For example, a more lenient manager may rate all their employees as fives because they met their goals and did everything the manager asked. In contrast, a more authoritarian manager may say that one employee who performed similarly did the bare minimum and evaluate that employee as a three. The employees did the same work and had the same outcomes, but one would be on track for a promotion and higher compensation, and the other wouldn't. Calibration ensures that everyone is operating from the same criteria.

Calibration enables accurate and fair quarterly performance appraisals without frustration. For too long, administrative constraints have limited the calibration process to a yearly activity. It was manual and driven by HR business partners, so therefore it was never able to be used throughout the organization—usually only for top leaders—sacrificing data accuracy and fairness. We believe the calibration process should be instantaneous so that you can perform precise, unbiased calibrations throughout the year. It's not being driven by HR, but rather managers can do it on their own. In addition, calibration aggregates rich performance data into clear, impartial insight into employee performance at a glance.

With that, you can make timely and fair data-driven talent decisions anytime, not just during the year-end appraisal process. Over time you can do the following:

- Dramatically reduce the time your HR team spends facilitating calibration sessions.
- Easily capture an employee's complete body of work when evaluating performance.
- Help your diversity and inclusion goals by being alerted to hidden biases in your performance process.

- Provide insights into company-wide performance for HR and leadership decision-making.

Regularly Reevaluate Your Compensation Strategy

We believe your compensation strategy is an ongoing conversation. You need to make sure you're paying people competitively. Also, it doesn't matter if everyone is working hard, doing great, and performing at an optimum level. If your organization is struggling, you need to evaluate the compensation.

A Case Study in Transitioning to Quarterly Reviews: Optimizely

Optimizely helps other high-tech, entertainment, retail, and travel companies optimize their websites while executing content marketing in new and different ways and releasing and optimizing new features. Optimizely is focused on innovation and helps other organizations innovate.

Optimizely's Erin Flynn,[12] a former chief people officer who now acts as an adviser and board member to many organizations, joined the company after serving as the CHRO for Salesforce for ten years. When Erin first joined Optimizely, it had no formal compensation review process. People could ask for feedback from as many people as they wanted, but the feedback was based on how they lived to the company values. It was not in any way focused on performance. Employees were mostly gathering feedback from their peers, which wasn't very useful information. So, Erin started to gather her own feedback and found out these employees wanted more "actionable feedback"—how they could improve their skills, develop more, or achieve goals.

As the chief people officer, Erin was asked to create and implement a compensation structure and conduct compensation reviews. Three months after being hired, she established this review process. Once that was in place, she was able to move and create a performance-feedback process. In addition, the head of engineering made it clear to Erin that, to be competitive in their industry, he needed to show candidates that they had an accelerated progression or potential for accelerated progression once they were hired. That information is key to engineers' decision-making—they want to know from the outset that they have a path forward in the company and that they won't just be staying in one position.

Erin set the performance-review process up as an annual review, but that only lasted a year. She soon realized that everybody in the company wanted one-offs—permission to review and promote throughout the year in order to remain competitive. She said, "We were chasing all these one-offs and trying to justify them, especially to their peers, and it made sense that we moved to a quarterly compensation review process as well as a quarterly feedback process."

Employees embraced the quarterly feedback process almost immediately. At one point, Erin reported a 97 percent participation rate. "People wanted the feedback, and the head of engineering, in particular, was delighted that they had the opportunity to show people an alternative."

At the time, Optimizely was a new kid on the block, basically a start-up with five hundred employees, and it was competing with the likes of Google, Facebook, Airbnb, and Uber for talent. But, Erin added, "We needed to attract and retain people who wanted to be with us for the right reason. And so showing them their career path from the beginning was helpful."

In addition to successfully recruiting, retaining, and compensating top talent, Erin found the quarterly feedback reviews helped with what she calls a "conceptual shift" within the company. Before she arrived, the reviews were tied to living the corporate values. Still, with quarterly reviews, the emphasis became more on how employees are contributing to the company's bottom line in their role.

All along, Erin knew that the intention behind the quarterly reviews would be that they would drive compensation and promotions. But she made clear from the outset and rollout that employees shouldn't expect a promotion every quarter or even every other quarter. Instead, it ensured that Optimizely's compensation remained competitive within its market.

Many things go into a compensation decision, including performance, but Erin wanted the flexibility to reevaluate compensation on a variable program. "If we introduced a new vertical they were going after in the middle of the year, for example, we needed to be flexible," she noted.

After every major compensation review, Optimizely would publish the results. It would measure the company's performance against the CEO's OKRs, as it did for every person in the company. All employees had objectives and key results, in other words, which they were measured against.

"This was something that was important to employees because there was a time when the founder didn't present results. People were working hard, but they didn't know what they were working toward," Erin explained. "So they didn't know what the executives were being held accountable to."

The engineers especially appreciated this, as they could receive and give feedback right in the flow of work through their Jira software. And the sales team could do so within Salesforce. That was easy.

Her team and managers worked together, so the reviews were no more than three questions. The employees would answer them, the manager would review them, and they sat down together.

Then all the managers went through the compensation review together and—depending on the area, engineering or sales—each manager had the flexibility to handle the process differently. For example, engineering might have an "all-hands" meeting to announce promotions or met goals, and a sales team might post things on a leaderboard. In engineering, Erin says, it's essential to show people there is an opportunity for movement.

And Optimizely would repeat that process. The company spread out its budget for the different quarter reviews. After each review, it would run calibration sessions—attended by various managers, directors, VPs, and heads of engineering. There they all discussed whom they wanted to watch. "Using Betterworks' calibration process enabled the conversations around talent that just frankly didn't happen before," Erin added. "And since there was now an opportunity to be promoted quarterly, you saw people giving their all in all situations."

Another unexpected positive outcome of increasing the frequency of feedback and promotion opportunities was that it impacted the business side. Erin explained, "Over time, the release cycle of our technology got tighter because we were optimizing our features. So, we were releasing more. When I joined, we released technology once a year and then moved to twice a year. Then we moved to four times a year."

This is important, especially to software engineers who might work on a product at Google for two years that might never see the light of day. Having employees able to see their work released out into the world is incredibly motivating. Erin added, "It was a big impact that was supported by the performance feedback cycle, the compensation cycle, and eventually the release cycle, which only became tighter and tighter and tighter. Ultimately, it drove results for the company. All of that performance feedback and moving to a quarterly process accelerated our transformation. It was fantastic."

Erin didn't face resistance in her organization or from HR in transitioning to the quarterly feedback and using Betterworks. Instead, engineering loved it, and overall, leaders loved it, because the company became more agile by moving toward performance enablement and real-time feedback.

HR loved it as recruiting tool to attract talent too. HR professionals told people, "You will actively receive feedback throughout the year and have reviews every quarter. And based on your ability to incorporate that feedback, deliver results, and stretch your goals, you can have an accelerated career here."

I Want It Now

We liken what happened in the workforce to what happened on television. For decades, we relied on three major networks that rolled out one season of shows—typically from September to May. We would have to wait until September for our favorite show to return. But, with the advent of Netflix and streaming services, viewers have come to expect multiple season releases in a year.

Television had to adapt because the market was demanding that— no one would wait anymore. And the mentality of people who stream is the same for those in the workplace. They want what they want, and, in the ineffable words of *Willy Wonka & the Chocolate Factory*'s Veruca

Salt—they "want it now." They are bringing that mindset to the workplace every day. They are, however, not coming from Veruca's bratty or entitled place, but rather from the same place that Viola Davis was coming from when she demanded the industry to "pay me what I am worth."

These employees know what they are worth. They also know what your competitors are willing to pay them and are prepared to leave if you don't pay according to their worth, but not before reviewing your company on Glassdoor. They don't have time to wait a year to find out what happens to their career. They want opportunities to grow, get feedback, and be rewarded—when they want them, not a year from now, but today. *Now* is the operative word.

So, *now* is the time to change. *Now* is the time for HR to *take* that seat at the table and demand these changes happen. The only way to do this is to recognize the following.

The Way We Work Is Changing

Your goals for your employees have not changed. You still need them to feel engaged, productive, and effective. You still want them to feel good about their work and their future with your company. And you still want them to turn that commitment into shared success. But everything else is evolving, especially in a postpandemic world—and fast.

Real Change Requires Commitment

Realigning around performance enablement—and making employees active participants in their development—is a different way of thinking. It means a shift from traditional, top-down goal management and one-way communication and will be an adjustment for many managers. Successfully implementing any real, systemic change will require a commitment to company-wide process adoption and change management.

Meaningful Employee and Business Goals Need to Be Continually Reset

A core part of good employee enablement is good goal-setting. When aligned with a larger team and company goals, individual goal-setting can be a key driver of performance—and when employees can take an active role in that process, they will be more engaged, productive, and successful. Set business goals from the top and use a comprehensive road map to help each team and individual align to those goals. Using a clear, accessible goal-setting tool helps employees see how their work directly impacts business results and provides critical feelings of purpose, mastery, and autonomy.

Systems and Processes That Promote Agility Need to Be Created

Keep goals flexible to accommodate changes in the business environment, and make it possible for employees to adjust goals to ensure they are always aligned with business needs.

The Compensation Strategy Needs to Be Reimagined

We've found that the best compensation strategies look beyond performance, ratings, and pay alone. Instead, they also look at the complete picture. An excellent compensation strategy considers current industry demands, the economy, and the needs of employees, such as the desire for remote work, flexibility, mental and physical health support, vacation time, stock options, and so forth.

Performance-Based Pay Magnifies Bias and Inequity

Performance-based compensation can get muddled easily, potentially magnifying existing unconscious biases. Performance management has traditionally been subject to all kinds of biases—recency bias, the horn or halo effect, along with race, gender, religion, age, and sexual-identity biases.

Intrinsic Motivators, Not Just Money, Influence Employees

You need employees to find their rewards in work itself. Whether being an active participant in workplace culture or finding learning opportunities embedded within daily tasks, intrinsic motivators drive more significant performance potential than monetary rewards. Having meaning and purpose, a sense of worth, and opportunities for growth and advancement are highly motivating. Feeling part of an inclusive and connected culture inspires employees as well.

Frequent Feedback and Recognition Changes Outcomes

Employees need a line of communication with managers to receive feedback and recognition in the flow of work. Regular feedback helps team members see how they're performing, which can inspire high-performing employees to take greater pride in their work. Don't underestimate the power of recognition. Performance-based pay is rarely as motivating as frequent feedback and recognition of work well done, even if the feedback is just oral. We've found the best way to *make* this happen is for CEOs to make a seat at the table for chief people leaders.

Key Takeaways

- Getting rid of annual performance-related compensation requires a switch to performance enablement. The best way to keep high-performing employees moving in the right direction is to ditch performance-related pay in favor of performance enablement and employee empowerment. The most critical aspect of employee enablement is helping employees see their work's role in driving business results. Performance-based compensation doesn't give employees anything to aspire to beyond rewards. *Performance enablement helps employees see what they're capable of and helps them achieve it.*

- You need to communicate your strategy to employees. Employees and management should feel comfortable having open conversations about compensation. Transparency from leadership—especially around hot-button topics like pay—is key to supporting better employee experience and job satisfaction. If you're no longer relying on performance-related pay to increase your employees' salaries, explain what criteria you're using instead. Help employees understand how rewards are distributed and how pay bands are calculated.

- Performance-enablement plans require quarterly reviews. The plans should coincide with company goals and align employee performance with business results. They should be implemented alongside goals on a quarterly basis and close with a quarterly formal review.

- Conversations around performance and compensation should be separate. After introducing quarterly performance reviews and creating a continuous feedback system, you still need to have conversations around compensation, but they shouldn't be held at the same time. Quarterly check-ins should be a place to establish forward-looking goals. Compensation conversations should be held periodically or as needed.

- A ratingless system and calibration meetings help to offset bias. If you are decoupling compensation from annual reviews, use calibration meetings to discuss employees' performances and agree on a uniform way to allocate performance bonuses and pay.

Conclusion

W E'VE MADE THE case to ditch your old performance-management process, including annual reviews, rank-and-yank rating systems, and cumbersome compensation strategies, and to replace it with more robust and agile performance-enablement tools. More important, we hope that we have convinced CEOs that the most important thing you can do as a leader is to elevate HR to a key position on your leadership team, because you simply can't afford not to.

In the next ten years, the workforce is going to experience a dramatic shift. Nearly 75 percent of the workforce will be millennials. Boomers won't be at the helms of organizations; Gen X will be taking over. They're not afraid of change, as they've been adapting to it their entire lives. And millennials and Gen Z behind them will not only expect but demand more engagement and continuous feedback. They are used to a world that responds to them, is in tune with them, and anticipates what they need. We live in a rapidly changing and hyperconnected world, and we've all become accustomed to convenience. We know what we want, how we want it, and when we want it—and that is usually right now. We don't just predict, we know: The primary driver for people in the workforce is wanting a simple and convenient performance-enablement tool.

Thanks to the COVID-19 pandemic, we've all been forced to reimagine and rethink what it means to manage employees—not just in our offices, in person, but at all times—wherever they are and whatever platforms they work in. The pandemic forced a needed conversation about what makes a company run—it's not just the innovation, not just the products, nor the bottom line. It's people. Without people, even the best companies with the best ideas will perish. If organizations don't realize the need to constantly invest in and develop their people, they won't have to wait too long to join the ranks of Borders and, in the most recent case, Twitter.

The most successful companies adapt, change, and grow with the times. But the *best* companies don't just focus on their customers, they focus internally on their employees. We've seen it over and over with our clients—Vertiv, Optimizely, Intuit, Udemy, Grupo Posadas, University of Phoenix, and many more. Happy, engaged, and empowered employees are what make an organization go beyond being successful to being truly transformational. If you want a great organization, you have to rethink and transform how you engage with employees. (Flip to the appendix for a few extra case studies.)

If you mean business about making work better, then we believe the first thing you need to do is make performance enablement your number one priority. If you're a CEO, hire a CHRO and empower the person from day one to start transforming how your employees engage with, and receive feedback from, their managers. If you're a CHRO, demand a seat at the table and make your voice heard. Reach out to us, and we'd be more than happy to help you present your case to the CEO or board. And if you're a manager or HR leader, you too can drive change. You say to your leaders or decision-makers, "This is what we need to make a real impact in our organization. We don't have time for annual performance reviews and cumbersome compensation strategies linked to annual performance reviews. We need more transparency, and we need to understand what the goals of the organization are and how we fit into them. How does my work contribute to the whole?" Tell them that it's important for leadership to see the transparent accomplishments of employees whenever they want and that employees can drive regular check-ins with their managers as much as the manager.

We've seen that the companies we've worked with perform better than companies that do things the old way. They're winning against their competitors, their stock is going up, and their revenues are growing faster because they have intentionally created environments where their people are working on the most important things and therefore have better experiences.

We believe managers should spend no more than fifteen minutes preparing the feedback to give to each employee during regular check-ins throughout the year. Moreover, it's important to change the culture around feedback so that it's transparent and aligned with both the employee's and the organization's goals. The happiest, most productive, and most empowered employees are those who see that their daily goals and activities contribute meaningfully to the entire organization's goals.

We know some companies think the solution is spending millions on software that tracks clicks on a computer and the time someone sits in front of the laptop, and some CEOs are advocating for "hard-core" practices—forcing their employees to work long hours with zero flexibility and threatening to fire them if they don't comply. These practices are myopic. In an effort to make short-term gains, they will burn their employees out, lose their trust, and drive them away. Ultimately, these practices breed contempt, create stress, and reduce productivity.

We believe that when there is an understanding between a manager and their employees on both personal and professional goals, they become more engaged and goal-oriented and know that their work matters and impacts the overall success of the company. Through interviewing twenty-five hundred people, we saw a 25 percent increase in engagement scores when people were using Betterworks. We also saw a 44 percent increase in their willingness to go beyond the standard job description (no quiet quitting here). In a world where organizations are struggling to keep employees, why not create an organization focused on the company's goals and outcomes while helping employees achieve theirs?

It is our deepest hope that *Make Work Better: Revolutionizing How Great Bosses Lead, Give Feedback, and Empower Employees* showed you how to create that organization. We hope we've offered you real, timely, and cost-saving solutions. Ultimately, we hope we convinced you to transform performance management into performance enablement so you too can have empowered workers who feels like they are really making a difference in their organization.

There is no time like the present to make work better. So get started.

What We Believe

A Changing World Demands a Reimagination

The world around us is changing at a disruptive pace. One unprecedented event gives way to another; navigating without a road map has become the typical mode of operation. And through it all, we keep daring to dream and build resilient businesses that endure. But the realities of these dynamic times call for a radical reimagining of work.

Our buyers have the power they may not yet understand—power to transform their businesses and the experience of work for their employees and power to drive business results and lead their executive teams successfully through transformation.

Talented and Engaged People

People are your most important asset. When they feel valued and invested in, they engage and bring their best selves to work.

Yet, the performance of those very people is to be managed, just like a cog in a wheel. Managers are asked to keep score, instead of inspiring and supporting them. And CHROs measure and comply but, unsurprisingly, see little result.

The best talent loses patience and goes elsewhere. Or even worse, the employees check out without telling you.

Remote and Hybrid Workforce

In 2020 you told employees that they are working remotely indefinitely. You asked them to show up in the most trying of circumstances: kids at home, illness, global conflict, existential crisis. But then productivity went up. Business performed. Now the illusion that work had to be done in an office building was broken. People valued newfound flexibility and realized they had actually always needed it. Now they expect it. Top talent demands it. When people can work from anywhere, and at any time, business benefits.

Work-Life Integration

You now call it work-life integration, which has displaced the age-old myth of work-life balance.

Engaged employees will rise to a challenge when they believe in your mission and in their leadership. In return, employees want to feel like human beings—have connection, purpose, respect, and appreciation. When those elements are absent, they ask, "Is this really worth it? For what am I working?" Employees know they're replaceable. Without an authentic sense of connection, true engagement is impossible.

Lives and Breathes Digital

Your workforce lives in a digital world. Yet digital transformation has not lived up to the need for employees and managers to experience meaningful connection, to both each other and those around them.

This connection is vital to alignment, coaching, and accomplishment. And employees are more than ready for solutions. Providing consumer-grade work experiences is the new norm for differentiating your brand and developing your talent.

Enterprise-Class Accessibility, Security, and Scalability

You've been inundated by promises from a new breed of software tools that say they can deliver employee engagement. But they didn't measure up to the complex needs of your business. As a result, the people didn't show up. Confusion led to frustration, and low adoption followed.

The right solution does not require compromise. It can support a dynamic workforce and workplace, comply with local and international regulations, integrate with existing and future investments, and keep data safe. Enterprise-class technology is the gold standard for driving sustainable change.

Strong Business Fundamentals

Shift to hybrid. Restructure. Focus on wellness. You've been asked to uproot and evolve just about every aspect of an HR professional's job in a matter of months, and sometimes days. And you did it.

But it didn't stop there. The new normal is disruption, which leads to business volatility and risk. As a result, leaders are looking closely at the business fundamentals—growth, the bottom line, product leadership, and solid customers—as the bedrocks to weather what's next.

Yet, it is a resilient and engaged workforce that achieves these outcomes.

Lead Back to People Fundamentals

HR leaders are overloaded, and some even feel powerless while they look for ways to unlock exceptional performance. Great managers engage, recognize, coach, and invest time and energy into employee development and growth—they are the leaders that employees never leave. Transformative HR provides executives long-sought insight into how traditional performance management is modernized to enable exceptional individual and organizational performance.

Make Work Better

Strategic leaders know that an engaged workforce is essential to a healthy business. You may have an incredible product, unparalleled vision, and the business fundamentals to dominate your market, but without people fundamentals, you'll never make it to the top.

An engaged employee feels heard, knows he or she matters, and understands the impact he or she has on the business. That employee brings their best to work every day, all day. A transformational manager knows how to connect business objectives to employee strengths and passion.

A business is a complex organism fueled by dreams, motivation, and relationships, but ultimately, it's made up of people who are bold enough to dream, people who are motivated to achieve, and relationships that can make the experience of work, at its best, transcendent. When great leaders have the tools they need to develop great employees, that's the moment when performance management becomes performance enablement.

The realities of these dynamic times call for a radical reimagining of work. What could work look like if we put people at the center of it? What if we stopped trying to manage people and started enabling them instead?

What if we tried to make work better?

Performance Enablement in Action: Case Studies

Case Study: Udemy

Industry: E-learning
Employees: 1,000
Headquarters: San Francisco, California

Udemy is an online learning course provider aimed at both professionals and students. Founded in 2010, the education platform now boasts over 155,000 courses, over forty million users, and over fifty-six thousand instructors. The Udemy Business platform is Udemy's professional-services education platform—trusted by Apple, Netflix, and Betterworks, to name a few—that provides users with unlimited access to the top six thousand–plus professional Udemy learning courses along with fresh content taught by more than fifteen hundred experts and real-world practitioners.

The Challenge

Like many start-ups, Udemy began as a small team of motivated individuals. "We started out with Small Improvements [software] for our performance management, but by the time our team grew to five hundred employees, we knew we needed a tool that would scale with our expanding team," said Cara Brennan Allamano, senior vice president of People at Udemy.[1] The company now boasts over eleven hundred employees worldwide.

The People team at Udemy wanted a platform that would help them transparently align their company's top goals to the goals and objectives of teams and individuals. The team also needed a platform that was easy to use and prioritized measurable data-driven objectives and key results.

"We'd done a good job of developing goal-setting practices within our teams, but we needed to take things a step further and connect our OKRs to align all of our work to the overall needs of the organization," Cara said. After six months of careful deliberation, the team chose Betterworks for its performance enablement.

The Action

"Onboarding with Betterworks was easy. The platform is intuitive, and we're a company that values learning and progressive change," said Cara.

The team enabled the Betterworks performance management, OKR, and transparent goal-setting toolsets. Now, all the teams at Udemy have access to company-wide goals, the goals of Udemy's CEO, team goals, and the goals of individual team members. Additionally, Udemy implemented a twice-a-year feedback and conversation cycle—using that time to assess the trajectory of the team and individual goals, analyze what adjustments may be needed to reach goals or personal-development milestones, and foster alignment and understanding.

The Impact

With Betterworks, the Udemy team now has full visibility into the company, team, and individual goals and is able to leverage feedback to align and support team members. "Because everyone has a high level of visibility, we saw a huge jump in platform adoption and participation. Now managers can see who is updating their OKRs, requesting feedback, and following through with their goals," said Cara. "Prior to adopting Betterworks we used to have about a 65 to 70 percent participation in feedback cycles; now, we're seeing a 92 to 93 percent response rate," said Cara. "Additionally, 85 percent of OKRs and goals are being met and completed in full."

Additional Information

Udemy is both a customer of Betterworks and a partner. The Udemy for Business integration enables L&D teams to provide customized learning courses that strategically align with their organizations' overall business objectives. Learners can search, discover, and launch Udemy for Business content from within the Betterworks interface and link course progress to relevant OKRs. Detailed course progress will be tracked back to Betterworks and is updated as a key result within an OKR.

Case Study: Posadas

Industry: Hospitality
Employees: 14,000+
Headquarters: Mexico City, Mexico

Posadas, also known as Grupo Posadas, is a hospitality company with more than 180 hotels and resorts operating under twelve brands in more than sixty destinations throughout Mexico. As the leading hotel company in the country, Posadas had over fourteen thousand staff members working in its hotels and over twenty-nine thousand hotel rooms across its properties. The corporation's roots date back to 1967. Through a series of mergers and acquisitions, the company grew and changed its name to Grupo Posadas in 1992, shortly thereafter becoming a publicly traded entity.

The Situation

Grupo Posadas is the top-rated hotel chain in Mexico and is ranked in the top ten for diversity, equity, and inclusion and as a "great place to work." In 2018, while developing its strategic plan for the next few years, Posadas recognized inefficiencies in its manual processes for performance, which relied on Excel and PowerPoint files that were time-consuming to develop and difficult to manage. The organization needed a faster, more efficient way to keep the team aligned on its mission to fulfill its strategic plan. Even after trying other performance-management solutions, Posadas continued to have issues efficiently communicating priorities and expectations to its workforce across the sprawling organization.

The Challenge

Posadas identified four key areas it needed to address:
- Disconnected teams
- Unclear priorities
- Lack of accountability
- Unambitious goals

The Action

Posadas created a matrix with goals, user experience, reviews, and other important factors to consider before deciding to implement

Betterworks in 2019. Previously, goals hadn't been clearly defined, and the organization was often misaligned on its biggest priorities. In implementing the Betterworks solution, Posadas wanted to create focus and accountability around these strategic imperatives.

Posadas began the program with just fifty users in the executive committee and corporate strategy team. The organization adopted an objectives and key results framework to support strategic management and execution, using Betterworks as the platform to enable performance and bring its strategic plan to fruition.

Posadas began holding monthly meetings to both support adoption of the Betterworks platform and promote understanding of the OKR methodology—how to define an objective, the importance of different team results, and the establishment of metrics, or milestones. These meetings focused on developing, reviewing, and improving OKRs throughout each quarter.

The Outcome

Monica Cabrera, manager of corporate strategy at Grupo Posadas, credits these metrics and the regular communication around them as a major contributing factor in the company's success, especially during the early days of the pandemic. As teams moved to remote work, she noted, these performance-enablement touchpoints were critical to help employees stay focused and build personal connections across teams.

Armando Smeke, head of strategic planning at Grupo Posadas, says Betterworks was able to help their teams maintain focus on company objectives even while experiencing major disruptions from the ripple effects of the pandemic. "When we started working with Betterworks, I thought it would help us with a lot of things, but I never thought it would help us with our mental health," Smeke said. "Everyone knew what to do to keep the company moving. One of the key drivers to survival was our ability to keep working and keep creating objectives."[2]

Posadas tapped Betterworks and OKRs to support a new product launch that was struggling to attain initial sales goals. "Betterworks has helped us [to] see where we are in relation to our goals, to pressure ourselves to think differently, and to be honest with ourselves," Cabrera said. "OKRs have forced us to think about those types of goals and see where we were underperforming. Betterworks helped show us we were not where we needed to be, and more importantly, to understand why we're not there."[3]

Posadas continues to build on its success with Betterworks. From its initial rollout to 50 users, the hospitality company grew its program to 550 users in 2019, now cascading strategic priorities to five levels under corporate. Internal surveys indicate that employees company-wide are impressed with the results, with more than 90 percent of respondents stating that they would recommend both the Betterworks platform and OKRs. Says Cabrera:

"At the beginning of the pandemic, weekly objectives, then monthly, then quarterly again, helped us keep the company moving. Everybody worked. Everybody aligned. To us, that is our great history with Betterworks. We can talk about sales or margins or some specific initiative, but these impact the whole company, and I think that's the most important."[4]

The Impact

After experiencing financial losses resulting from the pandemic, Posadas has achieved strong fiscal health. Its ability to remain agile and focused with Betterworks has enabled it to exceed its financial goals in the two years since. After surpassing last year's revenue goals, along with recent RevPAR (revenue per available room) increases of over 13 percent, the company expects to have a major reactivation of its core businesses this year, in 2023. The widespread adoption and prioritization of OKRs by 97 percent of users was a major factor in helping Posadas consistently exceed business goals.

As it prepares for the future, Posadas continues to explore additional opportunities to leverage insights gained from its partnership with Betterworks and is evaluating expanding its program to include conversations, feedback, and recognition.

According to Smeke, "If you talk with any of the members of the executive committee, they all would agree that Betterworks and OKRs are key for us to focus on the different priorities that we have. Everybody works. Everybody aligns. To us, that is our great history with Betterworks."

Case Study: Delta Dental

Industry: Health Insurance
Employees: 5,000–8,000
Headquarters: Los Angeles, California

Delta Dental is the largest dental insurance provider in the United States. It sells coverage to employer groups as well as individuals and families on a state-by-state basis through its national network. All of Delta Dental's holding companies and subsidiaries operate under the unified Delta Dental brand.

The Situation

Delivering smiles via dental insurance is a surprisingly tricky affair in the United States, where people move often and every state has its own rules. To operate in all fifty states plus Puerto Rico and other territories, Delta Dental has thirty-nine subsidiaries and thousands of employees who need to be cared for just as well as their patients.

Just like the nation, Delta Dental is remarkably diverse. The business is divided into many departments with their own established cultures and attributes, which don't always align. Divisions serving employers differ in habits and terminology from divisions selling to families, and there is even variance within states. This has led to friction between offices and degraded the company's ability to present a single unified front to customers, as well as to present an engaged and thriving culture attractive to both employees and new hires.

The Challenge

When leadership launched an initiative called Unite the Team, CHRO Kathy Claytor began looking for better practices around measuring engagement. The company was in the habit of conducting a single annual employee survey that took months to analyze, meaning news of issues came too late to address them. The survey also lacked granularity into offices and regions. Deeper insight, the leaders were certain, would provide the HR team with clues about how to culturally unite the company.

The Action

The HR team at Delta Dental looked at several different feedback and engagement solutions. The team ultimately found that Betterworks Engage was the only one that exceeded all of their criteria. It provided the HR team with a flexible tool for sampling employee sentiment on a more frequent basis. Here's what Betterworks Engage offered:

- Need for more actionable data → Real-time feedback
- Need to identify trends → Frequent surveys
- Need to report sensitive issues → Option to report anonymously
- Need to act on survey insights → Action plan and task-management functionality

The Outcome

With Betterworks Engage, the team was able to gauge engagement down to the individual meeting level, such as town halls. Periodic pulse surveys provided it with episodic data sampling, which allowed it to pinpoint trends and address emerging issues long before the annual survey was in. Using the software's task-management features, it was able to use the data to guide managers. For instance, when morale in certain offices seemed low, the team could investigate and create joint action plans. The platform would then track progress so it could verify that changes were actually implemented.

The Impact

The result was that Delta Dental's HR team got a bird's-eye view of engagement across the company and a dashboard from which to draw divisions together. Survey response rates averaged 85 percent in the first year, and manager action plans increased employee sentiment by 20 percent. People felt better understood and reported being better able to communicate with other departments.

The HR team also began to innovate. It developed a "regrettable turnover" metric centered around employee favorability ratings, which in turn gave better insights into recruiting and onboarding to ensure that messages aligned with company-wide culture and values.

With access to fast and accurate people data, Delta Dental took a big step toward uniting the team.

Case Study: Third Bridge

Industry: Finance
Employees: 1,500 across the globe
Headquarters: London, UK

Third Bridge is a financial management firm that uses research and narrative to empower investors and business leaders to make educated financial decisions. Third Bridge is headquartered in London, with offices in China, New York City, and Los Angeles.

The Situation

In an industry beset by declining fees and a rise in algorithmic investing, the financial management firm Third Bridge is still growing. In the decade following the 2008 recession, for example, Third Bridge grew from ten to nine hundred employees. The organization's advantage is its humanity, and it wears this badge proudly. The About Us page of its website begins with "We attribute our continued growth to the quality of our people and the skills and knowledge they possess."

As the company explains, those skills and knowledge are the result of constant internal feedback to the HR team about professional development. However, with increased size came new difficulties. New employees and hires brought an infusion of sometimes contradictory ideas, investment strategies, and security policies, which led to some employees feeling directionless. A sense of identity faded, and churn increased. Leadership and management realized that to know how to rectify the emerging issues, they'd have to first *understand* them. And for that, they needed data.

The Challenge

With its new initiative to gather people and performance data, management hoped to accomplish three things:

- To retain the company's existing talent as it continued to expand personnel and operations across three continents.
- To train junior managers and equip them to grow and advance their careers.
- To gather survey data without disrupting its many existing channels of communication, like Slack.

The training was needed to unearth and reinforce the values that had made the business great across geographies. Whereas those values were clear to some, they weren't clear to all. To reduce churn and prevent promising talent and managers from leaving, they needed clear paths to promotion within the company—and they had to know which paths would be valuable. And finally, the company needed a feedback system that adapted to its existing workflows, not the other way around. At its new size, it was unrealistic to expect employees to adapt to yet another system.

The Action

Third Bridge leaders evaluated several solutions and selected Betterworks Engage, which allowed them to send frequent, tailored surveys to different business lines or teams. They could standardize those surveys to benchmark sentiment in offices around the world, and they could provide opportunities for employees to give in-the-moment feedback. The survey plan looked like so:

- Geographically distributed → Multilingual surveys, local roles, and permission sets
- Need for detailed feedback → Custom surveys
- Need for ongoing feedback → Frequent pulse surveys
- Many ways to reach employees → Flexible surveys that work across channels
- Need to understand career expectations → Option for anonymous responses

Engage surveys are multimodal, meaning they can be completed within the company's existing channels, like Slack, or in the mobile app or from employees' desktop. Responses to the surveys were passed to the firm's HR management software, saving the HR workers time that they'd otherwise have to spend pulling data into CSV files and reuploading it.

In addition, Betterworks Engage provided clear reports that managers across the business could understand and act on. Third Bridge bosses and HR could then use this data to set action plans—a series of tasks aimed at creating the desired improvement. Reports also allowed the team to measure improvement based on what was getting checked off and whether it was on schedule. HR and management were able to review the data as a team and decide on the next best actions. The ability to provide anonymous feedback freed employees to say how they really felt. With more honest responses, management was better able to understand areas where career progression seemed lacking, in addition to the sorts of opportunities their employees were being offered elsewhere. Knowing about competing offers allowed managers to not only outmaneuver poachers and retain employees but also make their own offers to new hires more attractive.

All this led to a change in the training policy, in that managers earned more autonomy to select their career track. It also led to a more rewarding and better-aligned pay structure and inspired changes, like removing and reimagining some steps from the onboarding process, making it both shorter and more effective. With a firm grasp of which departments and individuals understood the firm's values, the organization was able to organize training around sharing between departments. Those values are now reinforced continuously, right from each new hire's first day.

The Impact

Third Bridge now reports having faster and more in-depth action planning, and pulse survey feedback feeds a virtuous cycle of positive change. Because of action planning, employees can see that management cares and thus feel more invested and more likely to respond. And when these actions visibly improve working conditions, like when management aids employees in planning their careers, it has become harder for them to envision leaving. Today, managers and employees report feeling more autonomy, and the churn the company initially experienced has declined.

Response rates to surveys are now 85 percent, far higher than the industry average of 60 percent. In some departments, it's as high as 98 percent. The very presence of a feedback mechanism, paired with clear evidence that it's being used to guide policies, shows employees and managers that leadership is employee-centric. That in turn inspires them to be more customer-centric. And that has helped the organization stay true to its foundational values as it grows and to remain great.

Index

abundance, mindset of, 57
action plans
    for bigger initiatives, 79
    creating efAfective, 67–68
    engagement and, 66–71, 77–79, 123
    measuring results of, 68–71, 77
    people development plans including,
        63–64, 66–71, 110
    quick wins to build momentum from,
        77–79
Adobe, 82, 90–95
affinity biases, 134
age biases, 134–135
agile companies and workforce, 41–42,
    61–62, 90, 95, 130, 144, 157
Amazon, 12–13, 118
anchoring biases, 135
Andes, Jeff, 36, 38
annual performance review. *See*
    performance management
Apple, 115–117
assurance, 21–22, 25, 26, 55
attribution biases, 135
    fundamental, 136
attribution feedback, 46

Beatty, Kate, 80–81
Bellow, Saul, 21
Bersin, Josh, 28–29
biases, 56, 120–121, 134–138, 149–150,
    158
board of directors, 94
Bold Culture, 134

bonus compensation, 7, 133–134, 145,
    149
Borders, 162
"Brook, The" (Tennyson), 105
Brown, Tina, 127, 132
Bryant, Adam, 91, 93
Burkus, David, 90

calibration processes, 120–121, 149–151,
    154
career development plans, 59–60. *See also*
    people development plans
cascading goals, 33–35
CBORD, 48–49
Chicago Bulls, 99–102, 107
Chowdhury, Sabrin, 143
Cisco, 31, 84–85
Clifton, Jim, 12
coaching
    culture of, 14, 31, 32, 50
    as manager want, 27
    performance enablement encouraging,
        32, 50, 124, 142, 146, 147
Coleman, Denis, 6
Colgate-Palmolive, 11, 107–111, 113
Collins, Doug, 99–100
compensation, 127–160
    bias and inequity magnified with
        performance-based, 134–138,
        158
    bonus, 7, 133–134, 145, 149
    commission-based, 144
    communicating strategy for, 145, 146

demand for reimagined strategy for, 130–132, 157

determination of, 128–129, 146

discontinuing performance- or merit-based, 141–146

as extrinsic motivator, 138–139

immediate need for changes to, 155–158

incentive programs and, 142–143

incentivizing wrong outcomes with, 133–134

inflation and, 130

intrinsic motivators vs., 132, 139–142, 158

key takeaways on, 159–160

pay equity in, 131

pay gaps or inequity in, 127–128, 131, 134–138, 145, 158

performance enablement-based, 141–142, 145–160

performance- or merit-based, 7, 11–13, 128–130, 132–139, 141–146

reasons to change approach to, 129–130, 132–139, 155–158

reframing as total rewards, 143–144

regular reevaluation of strategy for, 151

remote work and, 130–131, 140

timing of changes to, 35, 129, 130–131 (*see also* quarterly reviews)

transparency of, 129–130, 131–132, 145, 146

variable, 144–145 (*see also* bonus compensation)

competitive advantage, 61–62

confirmation biases, 135–136

conformity biases, 135

connection, 41–42, 57, 140. *See also* interconnection

constructive feedback, 47–50, 55

contingency feedback, 46

contrast biases, 136

conversations. *See also* feedback

people development plans facilitating, 65, 110

performance and compensation in separate, 149

performance enablement promoting, 44–45, 47–49, 110, 119

performance transformation with focus on, 80–82

COVID-19 pandemic, 4, 52–53, 127, 130, 143, 161–162

Creek, Katherine, 48–49

Cuban, Mark, 9, 14

culture

of coaching and feedback, 14, 31, 32, 50, 54

of connection and inclusion, 140

"culture fit" masking affinity bias, 134

of honesty and openness, 11, 30, 36–38, 80, 82, 145

as intrinsic motivator, 140

performance transformation by shifting, 80–82

of readiness, 49–50, 54–57

toxic, 11–13

data

action plan and engagement, 68–73, 77–79, 122–123

HR professionals' use of, 27, 33, 60–61, 78, 103

interconnected and integrated, 43–44

performance, visibility of, 120–121, 148–149

Davis, Viola, 127–128, 132, 156

development. *See* learning and development; people development plans

directive feedback, 46

Disney, Walt, 8, 14

diversity, equity, and inclusion (DE&I), 120, 138

Doerr, John, 118

DREAM (dynamic, restless, empowered, accountable, and mindful) goals, 48–49

Edison, Thomas, 9, 14
Eleven Rings: The Soul of Success (Jackson), 101
empathy, 22, 25, 26, 47–48, 54–57
employee Net Promoter Score (eNPS), 69, 80
employees
  action plans for (*see* action plans)
  annual performance reviews (*see* performance management)
  communication with (*see* conversations; feedback)
  compensation for (*see* compensation)
  development of (*see* learning and development; people development plans)
  engagement of (*see* engagement)
  organizational culture for (*see* culture)
  performance enablement for (*see* performance enablement)
  recognition of (*see* recognition)
  resignations of, 4–5, 62, 95, 130
  value of contributions by (*see* value of contributions)
  wants of, 26
engagement
  action plans for, 66–71, 77–79, 123
  bigger initiatives for, 79
  cost of disengagement vs., 37–38
  measuring results of, 68–73, 77, 122–123
  performance enablement supporting, 41–42, 57, 110, 119, 164
  performance transformation with, 77–81
  quick wins to build momentum for, 77–79
eNPS (employee Net Promoter Score), 69, 80

equity
  biases affecting (*see* biases)
  diversity, equity, and inclusion, 120, 138
  pay equity, 131
  pay inequity, 127–128, 131, 134–138, 145, 158
excessive leniency (or severity) biases, 136
executives
  CHROs as, 81–85, 88, 90–95, 102–103, 105–106, 162
  performance insights for, 121
  wants of, 28
exit interviews, 70
expectation biases, 135

feedback
  on action plans results, 68–71, 77
  annual (*see* performance management)
  attribution, 46
  constructive, 47–50, 55
  contingency, 46
  culture of, 14, 31, 32, 50, 54
  directive, 46
  empathetic, 54–57 (*see also* empathy)
  feed-forward vs., 34–35
  impact, 46–47
  as intrinsic motivator, 140–141, 158
  people development plans on, 65, 74
  performance enablement supporting, 41–50, 54–57, 106, 119, 125, 146, 151–155, 158 (*see also* performance enablement)
  performance transformation incorporating, 77, 95
  positive intent with, 54–56
  private vs. public, 110, 111, 112
first-impression biases, 135
Flynn, Erin, 151–155
focus groups, 69–70
Freeland, Grant, 92–93
fundamental attribution biases, 136

Gandhi, Neel, 143

gender biases, 138
gender pay gaps, 127–128
General Electric, 3, 6
Goldman Sachs, 6–7
Goodwin, Doris Kearns, 89
Google, 54–57, 117, 118, 154
Grant, Horace, 101
Great Depression, 19–23
Great Resignation, 4–5, 130
Grove, Andy, 118
growth opportunities, identifying, 63
Grupo Posadas, 162
guidance, 26

halo biases/halo effect, 137
Harter, Jim, 12
HCM (human capital management)
    systems, 123–124
home, working from, 130–131, 140
honesty and openness. *See also*
    transparency
    culture of, 11, 30, 36–38, 80, 82, 145
    Roosevelt's, 20, 22
horn biases/horn effect, 137
HR professionals
    CHRO position for, 81–85, 88,
        90–95, 102–103, 105–106, 162
    data use by, 27, 33, 60–61, 78, 103
    empowerment for decision making,
        90–93, 162
    HCM systems for, 123–124
    performance enablement by/for (*see*
        performance enablement)
    performance insights for, 122
    performance transformation role of,
        82–85, 88, 90–95
    return on investment in, 93–95
    strategic vs. tactical, 102–103
    wants of, 26–27
human capital management (HCM)
    systems, 123–124
Human Side of Enterprise, The
    (McGregor), 2–3

impact feedback, 46–47
implementation of performance
    enablement. *See* performance
    enablement implementation
*Impossible Presidency: The Rise and Fall of
    America's Highest Office, The* (Suri), 21
incentive programs, 142–143. *See also*
    compensation
inclusion, 140. *See also* diversity, equity,
    and inclusion
inflation, 130
integration, 43–44, 123–124
Intel, 117, 118
interconnection, 43–44. *See also*
    connection
interviews, 70
intrinsic motivators, 132, 139–142, 158
Intuit, 51–54, 118, 162
iPhones, 115–117
*Irresistible: The Seven Secrets of the World's
    Most Enduring, Employee-Focused
    Organizations* (Bersin), 28–29
*It's the Manager: Moving from Boss to
    Coach* (Clifton and Harter), 12

Jackson, Phil, 99–102, 107
Jobs, Steve, 9, 14, 115–116
Jordan, Michael, 99–102, 107

Katen-Narvell, Alex, 143
Kerr, Steve, 101
Kleiner Perkins, 118

leaders. *See also* executives; HR
    professionals; managers
    annual performance reviews by (*see*
        performance management)
    performance enablement by/for (*see*
        performance enablement)
    stakeholder wants of, 26–28
    traits of strong, 86–87
learning and development
    in agile companies, 41–42
    as intrinsic motivator, 132, 140, 142

learning management systems for, 124

people development plans for (*see* people development plans)

performance enablement making learning daily priority, 147

performance enablement training for, 50, 54, 106, 110, 147

resources for, 64, 66

strategic alignment with goals and, 53

Lincoln, Abraham, 88–90

Lindbergh, Charles, 22

LinkedIn Learning, 124

listening, 22–23, 25

long-term vision, 65, 105

managers

    annual performance reviews by (*see* performance management)

    coaching by (*see* coaching)

    empowerment of, 147

    PepsiCo's focus on, 106

    performance enablement by/for (*see* performance enablement)

    performance insights for, 121–122

    wants of, 27

McChrystal, Stanley, 89–90, 95

McGregor, Douglas, 2–3

McKinsey Quarterly, 3–4

meaning, 132, 139–140. *See also* purpose, shared sense of

Men's Wearhouse, 12

metrics, action plan results, 71

Microsoft Corporation, 5–6, 11

military, 1–2, 89–90

Morris, Donna, 90–95

Musk, Elon, 93

My Life in Full: Work, Family, and Our Future (Nooyi), 104

Narayen, Shantanu, 91

nonverbal biases, 137

Nooyi, Indra, 103–106

OKRs (objectives and key results), 49, 52, 80, 117–118, 141–142, 153. *See also* short-term objectives

onboarding interviews, 70

one-on-one meetings, 69

Optimizely, 151–155, 162

pandemic, 4, 52–53, 127, 130, 143, 161–162

peer pressure, 135

people development plans, 59–75

    overview of, 57, 59–60

    action plan development in, 63–64, 66–71, 110

    benefits of, 60–62

    career development plans vs., 59–60

    creating effective, 59–60, 62–65

    employee performance improvement with, 61

    engagement changes with, 66–73

    feedback provision in, 65, 74

    flow of work incorporating goals of, 73–74

    goal alignment and identification in, 64, 66

    growth opportunities identified in, 63

    key takeaways on, 74–75

    learning management systems vs., 124

    learning resources in, 64, 66

    long-term vision in, 65

    organization's competitive edge enhanced with, 61–62

    performance enablement implementation with, 110

    short-term objectives in, 65

    skills-gap analysis for, 62–63

    talent discovery with, 60–61

    template for, 65–66

    voluntary turnover reduction with, 62

PepsiCo, 103–106

performance enablement. *See also specific companies*

    benefits and characteristics of, 10, 32–33, 41–50, 147–151, 162–164

calibration processes, 120–121,
149–151, 154
cascading goals eliminated with,
33–35
compensation and, 141–142, 145–
160 (*see also* compensation)
connection and engagement with,
41–42, 57, 110, 119, 140, 164 (*see
also* engagement)
conversation promotion with, 44–45,
47–49, 110, 119
creating plan for, 146
current challenges for, 24–25,
161–162
definition of, 32
elements of successful model of,
147–151
empathy promotion with, 47–48,
54–57
evolution to, 28–39, 141–142,
162–164
feedback via, 41–50, 54–57, 106, 119,
125, 146, 151–155, 158 (*see also*
feedback)
foundations of, 41–50
immediacy of need for, 155–158,
162–164
implementation of (*see* performance
enablement implementation)
interconnection and integration with,
43–44
key takeaways on, 39–40, 58
people development plans in (*see*
people development plans)
performance management vs. (*see*
performance management)
quarterly reviews in, 35, 38, 144, 146,
149, 151–155
recognition provided with, 43, 45–49,
119, 125, 158 (*see also* recognition)
Roosevelt's historical, 19–23, 25
as scalable enterprise platform, 42, 125
(*see also* technological scaling)
stakeholder wants and, 25–28

strategic alignment via, 32, 33–35,
51–54, 104–110, 146, 148
training in, 50, 54, 106, 110, 147
transformation with (*see* performance
transformation)
performance enablement
implementation, 99–113
by Colgate-Palmolive, 107–111, 113
HR role in, 101, 102–103, 105–106
immediate need for, 155–158,
162–164
key takeaways on, 113
by PepsiCo, 103–106
reinvention as key to, 107–110
resistance to, overcoming, 109–113
strategy and tactics in, 99–107
by University of Phoenix, 36–39
voluntary participation in, 111–113
win-win outcome of, 107
performance management
changed processes except in, 15–16
compensation tied to, 7, 11–13,
128–130, 132–139, 141–146
cost of continuing old-style, 10–11,
94–95
focus of, 13–14
history of, 1–5
key takeaways on, 16–17
missed opportunities with, 8–9, 13–14
performance enablement vs., 10–11,
28–29, 38–39, 94–95, 141–142
(*see also* performance enablement)
rank-and-yank system of, 5–10, 13
University of Phoenix fixing, 36–39
performance transformation, 77–97
achievement of, 162–164
action plans for, 77–79
asking right questions for, 83–85
bigger initiatives and, 79
culture shift for, 80–82
engagement improvement for, 77–81
HR role in, 82–85, 88, 90–95
key takeaways on, 95–97
leaders embodying values for, 85–88

quick wins to build momentum for, 77–79
return on investment in CHRO for, 93–95
team building and teamwork for, 88–90
Performance with Purpose (PepsiCo), 104–106
Pippin, Scottie, 101
positive intent, 54–56
professional development. *See* learning and development; people development plans
promotions, as intrinsic motivators, 140
purpose, shared sense of, 22–23, 25, 26, 55, 139–140

quarterly reviews, 35, 38, 144, 146, 149, 151–155
quitting. *See* resignations

race biases, 138
race pay gaps, 127–128
rank-and-yank system, 5–10, 13
ratingless reviews, 149
rating systems, 2, 5–8, 12–13, 109, 129, 136. *See also* performance management
recency biases, 138
recognition
    as employee want, 26
    as intrinsic motivator, 132, 140–141, 158
    people development plans incorporating, 70–71, 73
    performance enablement supporting, 43, 45–49, 119, 125, 158
reinvention, 107–110
religion biases, 138
remote work, 130–131, 140
resignations, 4–5, 62, 95, 130
rewards programs, 143–144. *See also* compensation
Rodman, Dennis, 100–101

Roosevelt, Franklin D., 19–23, 25
Roosevelt, Theodore, 23

scaling with technology. *See* technological scaling
Seinfeld, Jerry, 9
sexual identity biases, 138
Shahid, Humera, 51–54
shared purpose, 22–23, 25, 26, 55, 139–140
short-term objectives, 65, 105
skills-gap analysis, 62–63
skip-level meetings, 78–79
small-group discussions, 69–70
social media, posting discontent on, 5, 128
stakeholder wants, 25–28. *See also specific stakeholders*
stay interviews, 70
stereotyping, 138
strategic alignment
    continual resetting of, 157
    of HR professionals, 26–27, 102–103
    as intrinsic motivator, 139–140, 141
    Intuit's goal-setting framework for, 51–54
    people development plans focusing on, 64, 66
    performance enablement supporting, 32, 33–35, 51–54, 104–110, 146, 148
    performance transformation with, 80, 83
    tactics and, 99–103, 106–107
Strategic Role Assessments, 7
Sun Tzu, 101–102
support, 26–27, 31, 38
Suri, Jeremi, 21–23
surveys, 68–69, 72, 77–78, 122–123

tactics, strategy and, 99–103, 106–107
talents, discovery of, 60–61
Team of Rivals: The Political Genius of Abraham Lincoln (Goodwin), 89

Team of Teams: New Rules of Engagement for a Complex World (McChrystal), 89–90

teamwork
  as employee want, 26
  as intrinsic motivator, 140
  performance enablement reinforcing, 55
  performance transformation with, 88–90
  recognition promoting, 48
  Roosevelt creating sense of, 22, 23, 25
  strategic and tactical approaches to, 99–102, 107

technological scaling, 115–125
  Betterworks software for, 117–121, 124
  employee engagement surveys and, 122–123
  key business system integration and, 123–124
  key takeaways on, 125
  leaders' insights with, 121–122
  performance-calibration process and, 120–121
  usability and, 115–117
  value of scalable enterprise platforms, 42, 125

technology
  performance enablement (*see* performance enablement)
  process changes and advances with, 15–16
  Roosevelt's firesides chats via, 19–21
  scaling performance enablement with (*see* technological scaling)

Tennyson, Alfred Lord, 105

Thorndike, Edward, 137

transparency. *See also* honesty and openness
  compensation, 129–130, 131–132, 145, 146
  culture of, 36–38, 80, 145
  performance enablement supporting, 36–38, 54, 121, 163

performance transformation with increased, 80
  radical, 11
  Roosevelt's, 20, 22

Trudell, Cynthia, 106

trust
  as employee want, 26
  performance enablement reinforcing, 32–33, 50, 55, 121
  Roosevelt creating sense of, 22, 23, 25

Twitter, 93, 162

Udemy, 124, 162

University of Phoenix, 36–39, 162

value of contributions
  employees wanting acknowledgment of, 26
  meaning and purpose with visibility of, 139–140
  mutual exchange of, 30–33
  performance enablement highlighting, 33
  recognition of (*see* recognition)

variable pay, 144–145. *See also* bonus compensation

Vertiv, 80–82, 162

Walmart, 16

War Department, U.S., 1–2

"War for Talent" study (McKinsey), 3–4

Welch, Jack, 3, 6

Wells Fargo, 133

Winfrey, Oprah, 9, 14

Wintour, Anna, 9

work-life balance, 144

Notes

Introduction

1. Gartner.com, "Gartner Says U.S. Total Annual Employee Turnover Will Likely Jump by Nearly 20% from the Prepandemic Annual Average," news release, April 28, 2022, https://www.gartner.com/en/newsroom/04-28-2022-gartner-says-us-total-annual -employee-turnover-will-likely-jump-by-nearly-twenty-percent-from-the-prepandemic -annual-average.
2. Kelsey Pelzer, "What Is 'Quiet Quitting'? Its Actual Meaning Is Not What You'd Think!," Parade.com, accessed August 23, 2022, https://parade.com/living/what-is -quiet-quitting.
3. Gallup, *State of the Global Workplace Report: 2022*, Gallup.com,– transcript and video, 2:36, https://www.gallup.com/workplace/349484/state-of-the-global-workplace-2022 -report.aspx#ite-393218.
4. Ibid.
5. Gartner.com, "Redefine Performance Management to Drive Impact," November 30, 2020, https://www.gartner.com/smarterwithgartner/3-steps-performance-management -delivers.
6. Nathan Sloan, Stacia Garr, and Karen Pastakia, "Performance Management: Playing a Winning Hand," Deloitte.com, February 28, 2017, https://www2.deloitte.com/us/en /insights/focus/human-capital-trends/2017/redesigning-performance-management .html.

Chapter 1

1. Lee A. Evans and G. Lee Robinson, "Evaluating Our Evaluations: Recognizing and Countering Performance Evaluation Pitfalls," *Military Review* (January–February 2022): 89–99, https://www.armyupress.army.mil/Journals/Military-Review/English-Edition -Archives/January-February-2020/Evans-Rob-Evals/.
2. Peter Cappelli and Anna Tavis, "The Performance Management Revolution," *Harvard Business Review*, October 2016, https://hbr.org/2016/10/the-performance-management -revolution.
3. Elizabeth G. Chambers et al., "The War for Talent." *McKinsey Quarterly*, January 1998, 44–57.
4. Greg Iacurci, "4.3 Million People Quit Their Jobs in January as the Great Resignation Shows No Sign of Slowing Down," CNBC.com, March 9, 2022, https://www.cnbc .com/2022/03/09/the-great-resignation-is-still-in-full-swing.html.

5. Robert Sutton and Ben Wigert, "More Harm than Good: The Truth about Performance Reviews," Gallup.com, May 6, 2019, https://www.gallup.com/workplace/249332/harm -good-truth-performance-reviews.aspx.

6. Joshua Brustein, "Microsoft Kills Its Hated Stack Rankings. Does Anyone Do Employee Reviews Right?," Bloomberg, November 13, 2013, https://www.bloomberg .com/news/articles/2013-11-13/microsoft-kills-its-hated-stack-rankings-dot-does -anyone-do-employee-reviews-right.

7. Jack Welch, "Jack Welch: 'Rank and Yank'? That's Not How It's Done," Opinion, *Wall Street Journal*, November 14, 2013, https://www.wsj.com/articles/SB10001424052702 3037896045791982810536735345.

8. Reed Alexander, "Goldman Sachs Layoffs Are Just around the Corner. Inside the Bank's Annual Performance Review, Which Helps Determine Who Stays and Who Goes," *Insider*, September 12, 2022.

9. Sutton and Wigert, "More Harm Than Good."

10. Kim Scott, *Radical Candor* (New York: St. Martin's Press, 2019).

11. Sutton and Wigert, "More Harm Than Good."

12. Jim Clifton and Jim Harter, *It's the Manager: Moving from Boss to Coach* (Washington, D.C.: Gallup Press, 2019).

13. Robby Brumberg, "The Demise of the Annual Performance Review Has Been Greatly Exaggerated," PrDaily.com, August 31, 2021, https://www.prdaily.com/the-demise-of -the-annual-performance-review-has-been-greatly-exaggerated/.

Chapter 2

1. Franklin D. Roosevelt, "Report on the Home Front," October 12, 1942, Franklin D. Roosevelt Presidential Library and Museum, http://docs.fdrlibrary.marist.edu/101242 .html.

2. Jeremi Suri, "How Presidential Empathy Can Improve Politics," *Washington Post*, March 12, 2019, https://www.washingtonpost.com/outlook/2019/03/12/how-presidential -empathy-can-improve-politics/.

3. Ibid.

4. Ibid.

5. Ibid.

6. Ibid.

7. Parts of this section have been repurposed from Jamie Aitken's speech at the 2022 Make Work Better Summit.

8. Parts of this section have been repurposed from Jamie Aitken's speech at the 2022 Make Work Better Summit.

9. Josh Bersin, "Enabling Performance in the Flow of Work," Betterworks, July 21, 2022, webinar, https://events.betterworks.com/betterworks/Improving-Employee -Engagement-with-Performance-in-the-Flow-of-Work?utm_medium=website&utm _source=events&utm_campaign=wbn-7-21-22-bersin-ondemand.

10. Parts of this section have been repurposed from Jamie Aitken's speech at the 2022 Make Work Better Summit.

11. Brent Skinner and Natalie Harrington, "Betterworks Helps University of Phoenix Replace Annual Performance Reviews with Everyday Performance Development," 3sixty Insights (website), August 10, 2022, https://3sixtyinsights.com/research-note-better

works-helps-university-of-phoenix-replace-annual-performance-reviews-with-every
day-performance-development/. Performance Development www.3sixyinsights.com.

12. Branka, "Employee Engagement Statistics—2023," *Truelist* (blog), last updated January 7, 2023, https://truelist.co/blog/employee-engagement-statistics/.
13. Ibid.
14. Ibid.
15. Skinner and Harrington, "Betterworks Helps University of Phoenix."
16. Ibid.

Chapter 3

1. Maren Hogan, "5 Employee Feedback Stats That You Need to See," *LinkedIn Talent Blog*, February 8, 2016, https://www.linkedin.com/business/talent/blog/talent-strategy/employee-feedback-stats-you-need-to-see.
2. This case study originally appeared on the Betterworks website. Betterworks, "How CBORD Created a 'DREAM' Culture with Betterworks," Betterworks.com, n.d., https://www.betterworks.com/cbord-case-study/.
3. Ibid.
4. Ibid.
5. This case study originally appeared in Betterworks's White Paper, "Managing Performance in a New Reality: Goals Matter More than Ever" written by Josh Bersin and Kathy Enderes.
6. Google, "Re:Work: Google's New Manager Training Facilitator Guide," Google.com, https://docs.google.com/document/d/16aDChcr2W6r683bCUeOD-4FEP3sx754_n37-bSHPFw4/edit.
7. Ibid.

Chapter 5

1. Jim Harter and Amy Adkins, "Employees Want a Lot More from Their Managers," Gallup.com, April 8, 2015, https://www.gallup.com/workplace/236570/employees-lot-managers.aspx.
2. David Burkus, "How Adobe Scrapped Its Performance Review System and Why It Worked," *Forbes*, June 1, 2016, https://www.forbes.com/sites/davidburkus/2016/06/01/how-adobe-scrapped-its-performance-review-system-and-why-it-worked/?sh=61028adf55e8.
3. Ibid.
4. Donna Morris, "The Strategic CHRO: Donna Morris of Adobe on Creating Value and Impact," interview by Adam Bryant, LinkedIn.com, April 18, 2018, https://www.linkedin.com/pulse/strategic-chro-donna-morris-adobe-creating-value-impact-adam-bryant.
5. Ibid.
6. Ibid.
7. Grant Freeland, "HR: From Paper Pushers to Game Changers." *Forbes*, July 2, 2018, https://www.forbes.com/sites/grantfreeland/2018/07/02/hr-from-paper-pushers-to-game-changers/?sh=731b030c6b74.
8. Ibid.
9. Morris, "Strategic CHRO."
10. Ibid.

11. Ibid.
12. Ibid.
13. Ibid.

Chapter 6

1. Indra Nooyi, in discussion with Doug Dennerline, December 1, 2021.

Chapter 7

1. There is no known record of him actually saying these words.

Chapter 8

1. Seren Morris, "Viola Davis Praised for Powerful Pay Gap Speech: 'Pay Me What I'm Worth,'" Newsweek.com, July 1, 2020, https://www.newsweek.com/viola-davis-praised -speech-pay-gap-viral-interview-1514644.
2. "Equal Pay & the Wage Gap," National Women's Law Center, n.d., https://nwlc.org /issue/equal-pay-and-the-wage-gap/.
3. Payscale, *2022 Compensation Best Practices Report*, https://www.payscale.com/research -and-insights/cbpr/
4. Ibid.
5. Ibid.
6. Parts of this section previously appeared in a post on Betterworks.com.
7. Invisalign, "First Impressions Are Everything: New Study Confirms People with Straight Teeth Are Perceived as More Successful, Smarter and Having More Dates," PR Newswire, April 19, 2012, https://www.prnewswire.com/news-releases/first-impressions-are -everything-new-study-confirms-people-with-straight-teeth-are-perceived-as-more -successful-smarter-and-having-more-dates-148073735.html.
8. Sabin Chowdhury, Neel Gandhi, and Alex Katen-Narvell, "Rethinking Total Rewards for the Post-COVID Era," McKinsey & Company, June 14, 2021, https://www .mckinsey.com/capabilities/people-and-organizational-performance/our-insights /the-organization-blog/rethinking-total-rewards-for-the-post-covid-era.
9. Ibid.
10. Ibid.
11. Ibid.
12. Erin Flynn in conversation with Doug Dennerline and Jamie Aitken, October 27, 2022.

Appendix 2: Performance Enablement in Action: Case Studies

1. This case study originally appeared on the Betterworks website. "Udemy Increased Feedback, Goal-Completion, and Transparency With Betterworks," Betterworks, September 23, 2021, https://www.betterworks.com/udemy-case-study/
2. This quote originally appeared as a part of a case study on the Betterworks website. "Grupo Posadas Achieves Ambitious Performance Goals and Exceeds Financial Targets With Betterworks," Betterworks, June 20, 2022, https://www.betterworks.com/posadas -case-study/.
3. Ibid.
4. Ibid.

About the Authors

Doug Dennerline is CEO of Betterworks, the leader in performance management software for enterprise companies. He has been working in Silicon Valley since 1982—starting with HP selling the first PC and minicomputers, followed by twelve years in the sales organization at 3Com, where he helped open up Japan and Asia while living in Hong Kong with his family. He spent twelve years at Cisco, massively scaling those companies as a sales executive. At Cisco, the company grew from 14,500 employees in 1998 to 48,500 employees in just two and half years. In his last role at Cisco, he became the CEO of Webex and the SVP of the Collaboration Software Group, post the acquisition of Webex by Cisco. He has been running SaaS companies ever since. He's worked for many famous leaders—Marc Benioff, John Chambers, Lars Delgaard—and learned many lessons about what it takes to grow and scale high-performing teams. Hint: it's not an annual review followed by a pat on the back and standard raise.

Doug was the president of SuccessFactors, which was the first company to move the performance management process to the cloud and was ultimately acquired by SAP.

As a father of three grown daughters, Doug is passionate about supporting and mentoring women in the workplace.

Jamie Aitken is VP of HR Transformation at Betterworks. Jamie helps customers reimagine the way employee performance is managed with proven systems and processes that work. She draws inspiration from her more than twenty-five years of HR leadership experience, spearheading organizational development, HR transformation, and employee engagement strategies that boost business performance. Her work as a consultant and an in-house HR practitioner spans the entire spectrum of human capital practices and multiple industries.

Jamie has a deep understanding of talent management strategies and principles, and has ideated and implemented global talent practices system redesign, strategic planning, and positioning in public and private for national and international organizations spanning all associated processes. As a McKinsey-certified facilitator, Jamie has also been instrumental in cultural transformations for several large enterprises—supporting fundamental change with her background in executive coaching, change management, and employee experience strategies.